# SHAKESPEARE'S HISTORIES

WORLD DRAMATISTS

# Shakespeare's
# HISTORIES

GEORGE J. BECKER

WITH HALFTONE ILLUSTRATIONS

FREDERICK UNGAR PUBLISHING CO.

NEW YORK

**Library of Congress Cataloging in Publication Data**

Becker, George Joseph.
  Shakespeare's histories.

  (World dramatists)
  Bibliography: p.
  Includes index.
  1. Shakespeare, William, 1564–1616—Histories.
I. Title.
PR2982.B4      822.3'3      76–15644
ISBN 0–8044–2032–7

His histories, being neither tragedies nor comedies are not subject to any of their laws; nothing more is necessary to all the praise which they expect, than that the changes of action be so prepared as to be understood, that the incidents be various and affecting, and the characters consistent, natural, and distinct. No other unity is intended, and therefore none is to be sought.

—Samuel Johnson,
"Preface" to his edition
of Shakespeare, 1765.

# CONTENTS

Chronology    1

Shakespeare's Age and Art    3

   1. *What Do We Know about Shakespeare?*    3

   2. *History and History Plays in Shakespeare's Day*    8

The English History Plays    15

  *The Life and Death of Richard the Second*    15

  *The First Part of King Henry the Fourth*    30

  *The Second Part of King Henry the Fourth*    51

  *The Life of King Henry the Fifth*    66

  *The First Part of King Henry the Sixth*    81

  *The Second Part of King Henry the Sixth*    94

  *The Third Part of King Henry the Sixth*    105

  *The Life and Death of Richard the Third*    117

  *The Life of King Henry the Eighth*    132

  *The Life and Death of King John*    146

The English History Plays on Stage    159

Perspectives    171

Bibliography    179

Index    185

# THE EDWARDIAN SUCCESSION: PART I

EDWARD III
1312–1377

1. EDWARD THE BLACK PRINCE
2. WILLIAM OF HATFIELD—*no issue*
3. LIONEL DUKE OF CLARENCE
4. JOHN OF GAUNT DUKE OF LANCASTER
5. EDMUND OF LANGLEY DUKE OF YORK
6. THOMAS OF WOODSTOCK DUKE OF
                        GLOUCESTER
7. WILLIAM OF WINDSOR—*no issue*

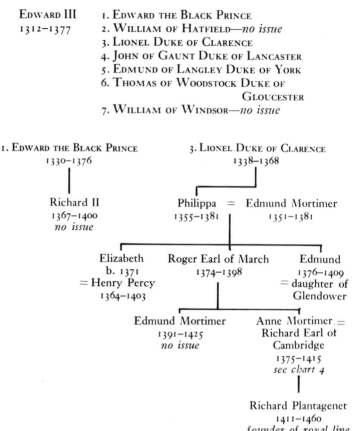

1. EDWARD THE BLACK PRINCE
1330–1376

Richard II
1367–1400
*no issue*

3. LIONEL DUKE OF CLARENCE
1338–1368

Philippa  =  Edmund Mortimer
1355–1381          1351–1381

Elizabeth
b. 1371
= Henry Percy
1364–1403

Roger Earl of March
1374–1398

Edmund
1376–1409
= daughter of
Glendower

Edmund Mortimer
1391–1425
*no issue*

Anne Mortimer =
Richard Earl of
Cambridge
1375–1415
*see chart 4*

Richard Plantagenet
1411–1460
*founder of royal line*
*see chart 4*

*Note: This genealogical chart is restricted to those
names that figure prominently in Shakespeare's plays.*

Blanch of Lancaster = 4. JOHN OF GAUNT = Catherine Swynford
　　　　　　　　　　　　DUKE OF LANCASTER
　　　　　　　　　　　　1340–1399

Henry IV　　John Beaufort　　Henry Beaufort　　Thomas Beaufort　　Joan B.　=
1367–1413　　Earl of　　　　　Cardinal　　　　　Duke of Exeter　　Ralph Neville
　　　　　　　Somerset　　　　　d. 1447　　　　　d. 1427　　　　　　Earl of
　　　　　　　1375–1410　　　　　　　　　　　　　　　　　　　　　Westmoreland

Henry V　　Thomas　　　John　　　Humphrey
1387–1422　1388–1421　1389–1435　1391–1447
　　　　　　no issue　　no issue　　no issue

Henry VI　　　　　　　　　　　John 1st Duke　　　　　Edmund 2nd Duke
1421–1471　　　　　　　　　　　of Somerset　　　　　of Somerset
　　　　　　　　　　　　　　　1403–1444　　　　　　1404–1455

Edward
1453–1471
no issue

1. Edmund Tudor　=　Margaret　　　　　Henry　　　Edmund
　　1430–1456　　　　1441–1509　　　　3rd Duke　　4th Duke
2. Henry Stafford　　　　　　　　　　　of　　　　　of
　　d. 1471　　　　　　　　　　　　　　Somerset　　Somerset
3. Lord Stanley　　　　　　　　　　　　1436–1464　d. 1471
　　1435–1504
　　no issue　　　　Henry VII
　　　　　　　　　1457–1509
　　　　　　　　　see chart 4

*See following pages for sections 5 and 6 of chart*

# THE EDWARDIAN SUCCESSION: PART II

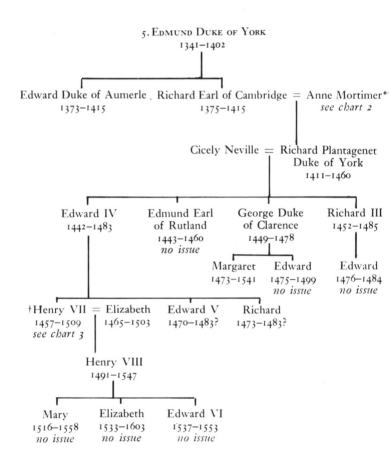

5. EDMUND DUKE OF YORK
1341–1402

Edward Duke of Aumerle
1373–1415

Richard Earl of Cambridge = Anne Mortimer*
1375–1415          see chart 2

Cicely Neville = Richard Plantagenet
Duke of York
1411–1460

Edward IV
1442–1483

Edmund Earl
of Rutland
1443–1460
no issue

George Duke
of Clarence
1449–1478

Richard III
1452–1485

Margaret
1473–1541

Edward
1475–1499
no issue

Edward
1476–1484
no issue

†Henry VII = Elizabeth
1457–1509    1465–1503
see chart 3

Edward V
1470–1483?

Richard
1473–1483?

Henry VIII
1491–1547

Mary
1516–1558
no issue

Elizabeth
1533–1603
no issue

Edward VI
1537–1553
no issue

* By this marriage the right of succession was brought into the
House of York.
† This marriage joined the Houses of Lancaster and York.

# CHRONOLOGY

1564     William Shakespeare is christened at Holy Trinity Church in Stratford-on-Avon on April 26; probable date of birth, April 23.

1582     A license is issued for marriage of S. and Anne Hathaway on November 27.

1583     Their daughter Susanna is christened on May 26. (She died in 1649.)

1585     Their twin children Hamnet and Judith are christened on February 2. (Hamnet died in 1596, Judith in 1662.)

1586–1590     S. removes to London and joins a company of players.

1592     S. is attacked by Robert Greene in his *Groatsworth of Wit*.

1594     The Lord Chamberlain's Men, a new company of players, is formed.

1595     S. is listed as one of the sharers in that company who receive payment for performances at court the previous Christmas.

1596     A grant of arms is made to John Shakespeare permitting him and his sons to call themselves gentlemen.

1597        S. purchases the property of New Place in Stratford.

1598        In his *Palladis Tamia*, Francis Meres cites S.'s accomplishments as poet and dramatist, listing twelve plays including *King John*, *Richard II*, *Richard III*, and *Henry IV*. An edition of Ben Jonson's *Everyman in His Humour* places Shakespeare's name first in a list of "Principal Comedians."

1599        The Globe Theater is opened on the Bankside.

1601        The Lord Chamberlain's Men put on an illicit performance of *Richard II* containing the deposition scene on February 7.

1603        The Lord Chamberlain's Men become the King's Men by royal patent on May 17, shortly after the accession of James I.

1608        S. becomes a one-seventh sharer in the Second Blackfriars Theater leased by the King's Men from Richard Burbage.

1610–11     S. retires to Stratford.

1613        The Globe Theater is completely destroyed by fire during a performance of *Henry VIII* on June 29.

1616        S. signs his will on March 25. He is buried in the chancel of Holy Trinity Church in Stratford on April 25.

1623        The First Folio, containing all his plays except *Pericles*, is published under the editorial direction of his colleagues John Heminges and Henry Condell.

# SHAKESPEARE'S AGE AND ART

## 1. What Do We Know about Shakespeare?

The short answer to that question is "not much." There is no major European writer since the Middle Ages about whom we know so little. What we do know is largely a matter of legal record: birth, marriage, and death in Stratford, deeds to various properties in London and Stratford, notations of payment from the royal treasury to Shakespeare as a member of various theatrical companies. There are also title pages of poems and plays bearing his name, and a few significant mentions of him by contemporaries. Finally there are the encomiums in the First Folio (the first collected edition of his plays, published in 1623), a portrait in that volume, and a bust of him over his tomb.

The rest is, alas, not silence but unbridled and unsubstantiated speculation. There have been many fictional reconstructions of his life and personality, such as Anthony Burgess's *Nothing like the Sun* (1964). These are made up out of whole cloth and reveal more about their writers than about their subject. A primary datum of the experience of literate men and women, William Shakespeare has in each age been recreated in their own image, shaped and colored by their prejudices and moral perspectives.

We have the date of his baptism, April 26, 1564, and we therefore celebrate his birthday on April 23, on the assumption that in his day baptism in the Church of England normally took place three days after birth. We know that his father was a man of substance, a town councillor, in Stratford, but that in William's boyhood he suffered reverses and came down in the world. We may legitimately infer that the grant of a coat of arms to John Shakespeare that the son secured in 1596 —that is, the right to bear the title of gentleman—was an effort to reestablish lost family dignity. There may, of course, have been no filial piety involved; it may have been merely an attempt to convey dignity upon William the actor and playwright by giving him gentlemanly antecedents, since it is quite possible that he smarted under the slings and arrows of neighborly condescension in Stratford and the low status of actor in London. We only know that he did receive the title of gentleman, that he did acquire important property, which permitted him to retire and die as a respected burgher in Stratford, though it must be admitted that after his death the citizens of that town evinced little pride or interest in him for more than two centuries.

We know that marriage to Anne Hathaway was authorized on November 27, 1582, and that a daughter Susanna was baptized on May 26, 1583. A pair of twins, Judith and Hamnet, were baptized on February 2, 1585, and Hamnet was buried on August 11, 1596. A whole mythology has been erected about the infelicity of this apparently forced marriage, on no more basis than the fact that the wife was eight years older than the husband and that he spent something over twenty years in London while his wife and children *appar-*

*ently* resided in Stratford. There is inevitably a countermythology, by which Anne Hathaway's cottage has become a shrine and the woman idealized as a queenly creature somewhere on the scale between Penelope and the Virgin Mary.

When and why Shakespeare went to London we do not know, or how he happened to attach himself to a company of players. He could have met such a company in Stratford and joined them on a provincial tour. He may have gone cold to London and made his debut by holding the horses of theatergoers, as legend has it. There is no evidence that he had any particular distinction as an actor. (There is a tradition that he played old Adam in *As You Like It* and the Ghost in *Hamlet*, both minor roles. His name appears at the head of the players listed in a quarto of Ben Jonson's *Everyman in His Humour*.)

At some early point he must have shown talent for writing plays, or for tinkering with existing plays, for about 1590, if scholarly dating is anywhere near the mark, he was a full-fledged, though somewhat mannered playwright. By 1592 he was sufficiently successful to draw envious and vituperative notice from another playwright, Robert Greene. In 1598 Francis Meres's *Palladis Tamia* hails him as the equal of Plautus in comedy and of Seneca in tragedy and notes his "sugared sonnets" that are circulating in manuscript among his private friends. Official documents of 1595 indicate that he was one of the sharers (coowners) of the Lord Chamberlain's Company. In short, after a relatively few years in London—certainly no more than ten—Shakespeare had established himself as coproprietor, principal dramatist, and occasional actor of the leading theatrical troupe in England. And he had made enough money to buy the handsome property of New Place in Stratford in 1597.

Shakespeare died in his native town in April 1616 at

the, to us, shockingly early age of fifty-two. It is reasonable to infer that he had been in retirement for
several years, since his regular production of about
two plays a year came to an end with *The Tempest*. It
is widely believed that *Henry VIII* and *The Two
Noble Kinsmen* were written while he was in Stratford in collaboration with John Fletcher, a popular
younger dramatist. We like to think of him as living in
ease and content in his native town, but for all we
know he may have suffered wracking illness in his last
years and have welcomed death. At any rate he was
buried in the chancel of Holy Trinity Church on
April 25, 1616. A bust was placed on the wall above
his grave, and there was a macabre inscription warning
against disturbance of his bones.

That he did not publish his plays during his lifetime
—he did see to it that his sonnets and narrative poems
were published—is not cause for particular surprise.
Plays were an ephemeral theatrical product; in addition it is likely that they became the property of the
company for which they were written. Actually some
of the plays did appear in print. Usually these were
unauthorized, corrupt texts—which we today call
"bad quartos"*—perhaps taken down in the theater by
shorthand or pieced together from actors' parts. Since
no copyright existed, unscrupulous publishers saw an
opportunity to profit from the popularity of a play.
Apparently, the theatrical company was moved on occasion to counter this by putting out a correct text—a
"good quarto."

It was not until 1623, however, that Shakespeare's

---

* "Quarto" and "folio" refer to the size of the page resulting
from the way a sheet of paper was folded. In broad terms, we
may think of a quarto as being the size of a modern novel or
biography, of a folio as being of the dimensions of a dictionary
or other type of reference volume.

plays were gathered together in an official edition, which we call the First Folio.* There are frequently significant differences between the folio text and that of the earlier quartos. Omission of scenes or change of order of scenes from one edition to another may be due to variation in production by the theatrical company. Minor verbal differences are frequently demonstrable printer's errors. For purposes of this volume, the problem of different texts is not unsettling, since the history plays are not plagued by many glaring divergences between folio and quarto editions, except for the omission from the quartos of passages considered subversive in Queen Elizabeth's time.

None of the uncertainties that beset our understanding of Shakespeare or his plays are relieved by the effort to ascribe their authorship to someone else. Players of this popular modern sport have put forward virtually every peer of education and renown living in England around 1600 as the "real dramatist," who, because of the social stigma of the theater, preferred to hide his light under the name of an uncouth Warwickshire hanger-on in the theater named William Shakespeare. These efforts arise from an inveterate snobbishness: How could the greatest writer in the English language be a person of no social standing, a man without a formal university education and wide social experience? How could so great a writer have possibly been so obscure a figure in his own lifetime? In sum, how could genius spring from the dung heap, and if it did so spring, how could it fail to illuminate itself and all around it? The only answer is that such genius did arise—we have the plays and poems, but very little else, to prove it. To ascribe this body of work to someone more in the limelight does not answer the fundamental question but merely provides a specious plausibility for the emergence of genius.

## 2. History and History Plays
### in Shakespeare's Day

However Shakespeare's apprenticeship developed, at an early date he began writing plays, trying his hand almost simultaneously at three different types of drama. Sometime around 1590 he wrote *A Comedy of Errors*, strict classical comedy; *Titus Andronicus*, strict Senecan tragedy; and *Henry VI*, a series of chronicle plays. It is in the last type that he showed the most interest and made the greatest initial development. The ten plays that he wrote in this genre are certainly not his greatest, but they are among the most interesting for their variety and for their technical virtuosity. With the exception of the two parts of *Henry IV*, which are composed on essentially the same pattern, no two of these plays are alike. They are varied and original in format precisely because there were no rules and very little precedent for this kind of drama.

In 1590 at least two English history plays were already in existence. They were *The Famous Victories of Henry V* and *The Troublesome Reign of John, King of England*. Shakespeare knew and made use of both of them in his plays about those monarchs. Unless other plays of this kind existed of which we have no record, there was clearly no established genre of the history play. Thus, though we cannot say that Shakespeare invented it, we certainly can conclude that he was the dramatist who gave it firm development and established it in popular favor. Of the twenty-one plays ascribed to him during the last decade of the century, nine were histories (and *The Merry Wives of Windsor* was a comic offshoot of those histories). Comparable dramas—such as the anonymous *True Tragedy of Richard III* (published in 1594 but probably written earlier) and Christopher Marlowe's *Edward II* (1593)—would seem to be on the pattern Shakespeare was establishing and to be competitors, not progenitors, of his early and popular work. Many later history plays by others are evident attempts to capitalize on his successes.

The history play offered a mixed public a theatrical experience that was new and satisfying. It appealed to the audience's appetite for historical fact (and legend), to its patriotism, and to its need to find moral order beneath the shifting and often catastrophic play of political forces. It was a well-established Renaissance belief that the function of literature was to delight and instruct. Nowhere could instruction be more effectively equated with delight than on the stage. There storied kings and warriors could be seen in the flesh; there the poignant passages of history could be re-enacted; there the splendor of the past could be made visible by pageantry and ritual.

The civil war of the fifteenth century—what we call the War of the Roses—was about as far removed in time from the English populace of 1590 as the American Civil War is from us today. Once events that are traumatic in experience are safely past, they become the material of legend, objects of curiosity, occasion for partisanship and debate. Americans have for decades been able to satisfy their curiosity through a deluge of books about their Civil War. The Elizabethans could not. Thus, when Shakespeare and others after him undertook to dramatize their history, the public responded with avidity. For the illiterate majority of the audience, this was their first introduction to their own history except for the bits and pieces that had come to them through oral tradition.

It was only in Shakespeare's day that a strong sense of national identity emerged in England. An immediate spur to English patriotism was the defeat of the Spanish Armada in 1588. The tiny island state had defeated the most powerful nation in the world and was secure from further assault after decades of anxiety. More important in the long run was the fact that England had finally severed her ties with Europe. Establishment of the Church of England—a national church—freed her from the power of the international Roman church, though the latter intrigued mightily to bring England back into the fold. In 1558 Calais fell to the French. For almost 500 years—ever since the Norman Conquest in 1066—English power and attention had been divided between England and France. For all practical purposes, dominion of the land across the Channel ended in 1453, but the fall of Calais was a symbolic termination and marked a shift in direction of English energies.

Shakespeare's histories reflect these changes by a kind of spontaneous chauvinism. Even as they depict the loss of an overseas empire they celebrate England's insular identity. (It should be noted that *King John* shows the last successful invasion by foreign troops.) The great poetic passages in *King John, Richard II*, and *Henry V* are an affirmation of English greatness. England must be English, these plays seem to say. There is no profit in involvement with foreigners, who are untrustworthy, cowardly, and effete. In all the history plays, the French, whether as antagonists or allies, are always fair game for ridicule as less than human, or at any rate less than English. In general, there seems to be a kind of patriotic imperative to impeach the manners, morals, and military capacity of the French.

The moral instruction the history plays afford is

directly connected with the purposes of history as they were understood in the sixteenth century. It was in effect "official" history with the object of propagating right religious doctrine and right political doctrine. The publication of emphatically dissident views is inconceivable. Early in his reign, Henry VII, the first Tudor and Queen Elizabeth's grandfather, began to encourage a presentation of past events favorable to himself. His interest was twofold: to trace his antecedents through his Welsh forebears back to the legendary King Arthur (he even named his first son Arthur), and to view the Tudor reconciliation as a far-off divine event toward which the course of history had inevitably moved. Both these purposes had their impact on Elizabethan literature, but it is the second that provided the shaping force for Shakespeare's history plays.

The immediate concern of Henry VII was to blacken the defeated Yorkists, especially Richard III. The various histories written during Henry VII's reign, and that of Henry VIII, achieved that effect. Of particular importance was Sir Thomas More's history of Richard III, which turned that king into a monster, and Edward Hall's *The Union of the two noble and illustre Families of Lancaster and Yorke* (1548), which saw in "the godly matrimony" of Henry VII and Elizabeth of York "the final end of all dissensions, titles and debates." Later in the century Raphael Holinshed's *Chronicle* incorporated the material of these predecessor historians. A second edition in 1587 was the principal source on which Shakespeare relied in writing his history plays. Indeed, Shakespeare often drew directly from it, merely turning into blank verse the speeches that Holinshed had invented for important personages.

What is significant is that Shakespeare accepted

these materials uncritically. He was a playwright, not a historian. Like almost all his contemporaries, he was not accustomed to weighing evidence from many sources. The printed page carried automatic authenticity, or at any rate he was only interested in what the printed page provided in the way of dramatic materials. Though his view of past events is that established by the official line, it is incorrect to assert, as many have done, that he was a (paid?) propagandist for the Tudor monarch, or even that he sought favor, or safety, by sedulously adhering to a view of the past that was pleasing to the queen and her ministers. Cautious he may have been. Having brought Henry VII to the throne in an aura of sanctity at the end of *Richard III*, he left the Tudors alone until he wrote *Henry VIII*, almost a decade after Queen Elizabeth's death, and even then he raised no inconvenient questions about Henry VIII's character or abilities.

In general, Shakespeare avoided the dangerous terrain of the Reformation and of contemporary political events. He appears to have been, by later standards, a conservative in respect to institutional arrangements. He did not question the institution of monarchy; he actively espoused the doctrine of social subordination, that is, of a social hierarchy in which men and women should be content to carry out those duties and to accept that station to which God had called them. He was, in other words, a writer of plays who, during part of his career, in response to popular demand or his own predilections, or both, made dramatic capital of the materials of recent, but not contemporary, history.

One qualification of this statement is in order. Historical materials when they appear in literature often serve as commentary on the present. To use a favorite Elizabethan metaphor, they are a mirror in which, ignoring differences of detail, the public may discern the main lineaments of a contemporary situation or problem. This may be no more than literary playfulness, a kind of puzzle, the equivalent of a *roman à clef*. Or this may be a deliberate safeguard. In absolute monarchies or dictatorships, it is dangerous to state the truth about conditions or policy without resort to some sort of concealment. Writers and readers alike perceive the advantage of such historical or literary analogy, generally considerably more subtle than Hamlet's use of a self-evident parallel to catch the conscience of a king.

There is no doubt that Elizabethans wrote and thought in this way. What better evidence can we have than Queen Elizabeth's outburst (when she was threatened by the Earl of Essex's rebellion): "Know ye not that I am Richard II?" But direct commentary was not Shakespeare's way. Contemporary allusions, yes, to titillate the audience with the possibility of more extensive contemporary application; exposition of problems of politics and leadership in past times that are still present under the queen; but no direct, sustained, organized mirroring of the present in the past, even when the sources from which he drew had such a pattern. The closest he came to doing this is in *King John*, which in a very general way suggests a parallel between Arthur and Mary Queen of Scots and between the invading French and the Spanish Armada, but does not provide any one-to-one correspondence.

We are bound to wonder what kind of impression the history plays made on their original audiences. What images of truth did they impose on the spectators' minds? We can speculate that for many the plays were primarily patriotic spectacle—and where comic scenes appeared, mere horseplay. The audience satisfied an uncritical curiosity about the past as they saw heroes and villains brought to life in actions that were part of the national legend. The names of Talbot, Warwick, and Henry V, for example, had an epic ring. Richard III was an exciting monster, a name with which to quell refractory children.

There would also be more sophisticated viewers who listened to the insistent emphases of the words and action and pondered their meaning in relation to basic problems of governance and civil order. These people would take away with them a strong impression of the costs of civil war, the dangers of disputed succession to the crown, the need for a strong monarch, and the perils that lurked in papish lands across the narrow sea. They would weigh the rights and wrongs of the actions of various kings, taking sides perhaps with Richard II or Bolingbroke. They would not notice, and they would not care, that the data of history were often manipulated for the sake of the drama, and that shadings of character were left out in order to sharpen the contrast between good and evil. They would accept what they saw as authentic history and would relish it both for its spectacle and for what it contained of right political doctrine.

# THE ENGLISH HISTORY PLAYS

## The Life and Death of Richard the Second

As is the case in all tightly constructed plays, the action in *Richard II* is only the tip of the iceberg, the culmination of past events and experiences that have brought the characters to the crisis that makes up the drama.

Richard of Bordeaux—he was born in that city while his father Edward the Black Prince was governing the English territories in southwestern France— had the misfortune to become king in 1377, at the age of ten, because of the untimely death of his father a few months before King Edward III died. Three of

---

The plays are presented here in historical order, not in order of composition, since they provide a fairly continuous dramatic account of events from the last months of Richard II's reign to the death of Richard III eighty-six years later and are thematically interrelated. *King John*, an early play, is without attachments to the rest of the histories and is therefore placed at the end of the volume.

Because they were written first, the three parts of *Henry VI* and *Richard III* are referred to as the first tetralogy. *Richard II*, the two parts of *Henry IV*, and *Henry V* make up the second tetralogy. Leaving out *Richard II*, scholars often refer to the other three plays in the second tetralogy as the "Henriad," that is, the epic of Prince Hal/King Henry V.

Edward's sons were alive: John of Gaunt, Duke of Lancaster; Edmund of Langley, Duke of York; and Thomas of Woodstock, who later became Duke of Gloucester. As men of rank and royal blood, they were conscious of their high destiny and none too cooperative during Richard's first years as king. Thomas of Gloucester, in particular, who headed the war party that was eager to continue the war for conquest of France, harassed the young monarch in every possible way. Eventually, in alliance with the Earl of Arundel and the Earl of Salisbury, and with the support of Henry Bolingbroke, John of Gaunt's oldest son, and Thomas Mowbray, Gloucester in effect took over rule of the kingdom. He forced Richard to dismiss his closest advisors, to allow their trial for treason, and to assent to their execution when they were convicted.

Richard never forgot this humiliation but bided his time. Some ten years later, when he learned of a plot led by Gloucester to depose him, he moved swiftly. The Earl of Arundel was tried and executed in September 1397. The Duke of Gloucester was imprisoned in the English fortress at Calais, where after a decent interval word was given out that the duke was dead. Mowbray, who had come over to the king's side, was governor of the fortress. He probably had Gloucester murdered at Richard's orders.

From this point on, events moved swiftly. Bolingbroke brought charges of treason and misfeasance against Mowbray in April 1398. This is the point at which the play begins. Unable to control the two nobles, Richard adjourned the trial and ordered a trial by combat at Coventry in August (I, iii). Suddenly, as the ritual joust was about to begin, Richard broke it off and settled the problem by banishing both contestants—Mowbray for life and Bolingbroke for ten years (almost immediately reduced to six years to appease John of Gaunt). Bolingbroke made his way to the Continent. John of Gaunt died in February 1399, and Richard committed an unpardonable error by confiscating all of Gaunt's property, denying Bolingbroke his rights to land and titles as the oldest son. This was excuse enough for ambitious Bolingbroke to come back to England and raise an army, ostensibly only to secure that which was his by right.

Meanwhile, Richard, who was no warrior, committed a second error. He made his ineffective and indecisive uncle, the Duke of York, regent while he led an army to Ireland on a punitive expedition. He was away from England for two months. During that time Bolingbroke landed in Yorkshire in early July and gained wide support, especially from the powerful Percy family in the north. The king's chief counselors fled but were captured and executed. Even the Duke of York deserted the king. Thus when Richard returned from Ireland to Wales in mid-August, he found himself without support. He gave himself up to Bolingbroke at Flint Castle on August 18, was conveyed to the Tower of London on August 31, and was deposed by Parliament on September 30. He was moved to the castle of Pontrefact in the north a month later and died there early in 1400, killed by Piers Exton, an eager sycophant of the new king. Bolingbroke, now Henry IV, vowed a pilgrimage to the Holy Land in expiation of this crime.

Only one of the major characters in the play is pure invention. Richard's second wife, Isabel, was only ten years old when he was deposed. She had been brought to England to be educated in English ways at Windsor. Richard never saw her again after saying goodbye to her there in June before going to Ireland. The other characters are all drawn from history with appropriate emphases to bring out the basic conflict of the play. Shakespeare created a Richard II who is not out of line with Holinshed's description, though he is much more complex:

> He was seemly of shape and favor, and of nature good enough, if the wickedness and naughty demeanor of such as were about him had not altered it.
>
> His chance verily was greatly infortunate, which fell into such calamity, that he took it for the best way he could devise to renounce his kingdom, for the which mortal men are accustomed to hazard all they have to attain thereunto. . . . He was prodigal, ambitious, and much given to the pleasure of the body . . . there reigned abundantly the filthy sin of lechery and fornication, with abominable adultery, specially in the king.

The lechery is played down by Shakespeare, but there is frequent mention of the unwholesome influence of his favorites—the gilded youth of the time.

The play has a simple design, reinforced in a number of ways both overt and subtle. The subject is simply the fall of one king and the rise of another. This automatically entails a contrast between the two, bidding the audience contemplate their strengths and weaknesses and by implication to evaluate their suitability for kingship. Insofar as possible, the play gives dramatic evidence of the weakness of the descending king and the strength of the ascending one. Where that is not possible, there is less satisfactory resort to simple exposition. Lest the design of the play be missed, certain images of this up-and-down movement are introduced, reiterated, and finally visually acted out in III, iii, where Richard is forced literally to descend to the courtyard of the castle, and Bolingbroke by this show of power figuratively rises above him.

The Richard whom we see at the beginning of the play is only an animated icon, a resplendent figure frozen in ritual and formality. He is so supported by form that he has never had to question his role or his suitability for it, or to examine his inner being. His position as king is essentially depersonalized, or impersonalized. He is far removed from his subjects and has no direct human relationship with them. He likes this formality, depends on it, and is helpless without it. This is the impression to which the first and third scenes lead, visually as well as conceptually. Ideal staging presents Richard, a figure as resplendent as the sun, raised in isolation above the court. It is not mere petulance that leads him to say to obstreperous Bolingbroke and Mowbray:

> We were not born to sue but to command.
>
> (I, i, 196)

Richard literally cannot conceive of any other way of being.

These early scenes by their very excess contain a covert mockery of Richard's attitude as well as a demonstration that formality without force is empty. Richard cannot control Bolingbroke and Mowbray; he cannot allow the trial by combat to be carried out. He gives disproportionate terms of banishment and under pressure remits part of one of them. He is petty about Bolingbroke's apparent popularity and quick to be suspicious of his cousin Aumerle for having showed courtesy to Bolingbroke. Later on, he is without sympathy for dying John of Gaunt, greedy to expropriate his property, and cavalier in the taxation he allows to be levied for his Irish war. The total picture is one of narcissism and arrogance. He does not govern; he basks in his own glory.

Even when he finds himself without an army, at the mercy of Bolingbroke's power, he still has faith in the sacredness of kingship:

> Not all the water in the rough rude sea
> Can wash the balm off from an anointed king.
> The breath of worldly men cannot depose
> The deputy elected by the Lord.
> For every man that Bolingbroke hath pressed
> To lift shrewd steel against our golden crown,
> God for his Richard hath in heavenly pay
> A glorious angel.
>
> (III, ii, 54–61)

He becomes aware of the hollowness of his ceremonial role only when, confronted by Bolingbroke's false obeisance at Flint Castle, he says to his kneeling cousin:

> Fair cousin, you debase your princely knee
> To make the base earth proud with kissing it.
> Me rather had my heart might feel your love
> Than my unpleased eye see your courtesy.
> Up, cousin, up! Your heart is up, I know,
> Thus high at least [as he touches his own
>       head], although your knee be low.
>
> (III, iii, 190–95)

When his kingly visage no longer commands awe and obedience, when for the first time Richard is forced to evaluate his role without preconceptions, his response is emotional and undisciplined, histrionic, in fact. It is from this point on that there is danger of idealizing him beyond what the text will support, of redeeming him as a man by purging him of false perception, in short, of turning him into a tragic figure. In fact, he toys with words to blur the meaning of his experience. He plays a role before Parliament, where he is called upon publicly to acknowledge his misdeeds, asking for a mirror so that he can look for physical evidence of his decline, then shattering the glass upon the floor. He goes to his grave embittered, passionate, still not fully understanding what has happened to him. Moreover, his gradual humanization in scenes with the queen, with a groom who talks to him about his horse, and with his jailors does not wash away his responsibility for failure as a king. The lineal successor of Edward III and the illustrious Black Prince, without blemish to his title, Richard has muffed it and thereby opened up the path to illegitimate succession and consequent civil conflict.

Bolingbroke, the ascending figure in the pattern, is not as subtle a character as Richard, but he is by no means a stereotype. His strength—and potential limitation—lies in the fact that his approach is pragmatic. The whole question of how Bolingbroke, against all precedent in a divine-right monarchy, managed to assume the throne is critical to an understanding of the man and the play. The simplest way of answering it is that Bolingbroke was a practical man, not greatly concerned with the niceties of feudal law and custom. He was in the right place at the right time and skillfully rode the wave of opportunity. Finding a power vacuum, he filled it without hesitation.

It is necessary in the play that his character be established at once. Somehow through the obscuring verbal formality of the opening scene we must discern that he is really challenging the king, not Mowbray. His protestations of loyalty and moral outrage are fulsome to the point of insincerity. Richard is aware of this when he says in an aside:

How high a pitch his resolution soars!

(I, i, 109)

Richard is also aware that Bolingbroke has been court-
ing the common people, that there is a publicly dis-
cerned contrast between Richard's aloofness and his
cousin's common touch. Richard commands obedience
—when he can get it. Bolingbroke attracts admiration
and loyalty by the apparent openness of his nature and
by the competence with which he controls circumstances.

In the latter part of the play, it becomes evident that
Bolingbroke as King Henry IV has the virtues in
which Richard has been shown to be lacking. He deals
directly and efficiently with the conspiracy in which
Aumerle is involved, knowing whom to punish and
whom to pardon. Thought does not inhibit action, nor
does emotion cloud his understanding of practical issues. To tell the truth, in his efficiency he is not very
interesting, or rather he becomes interesting only
when as king he has to face the ambiguities of experience. Even then, confronted with the murder of Richard, he seems to think that simple expiation will ex-
punge the crime.

The issue, then, is fairly joined on a simple pragmatic level. If the legitimate king, deriving his powers
from God, is a bad ruler, and a claimant, royal but not
in the direct line, appears to be good, what is to be
done about it? Is not the well-being of the kingdom of
more importance than the maintenance of strict legitimacy? Should not a weak king be removed so that a
strong one may rule? In terms of political expediency,
the answer seems to be a resounding yes, even though
Richard rises in our estimation when he becomes a
private person and Bolingbroke falls as we see him
investing himself in his own kind of insensitive formality.

However, even within the dramatic action pragmatic values are not allowed full sway. After Richard, the chief voice in defense of legitimacy is the Bishop of Carlisle, who risks his life to challenge Bolingbroke's assumption of the crown:

> What subject can give sentence on his king?
> And who sits here that is not Richard's subject?
> Thieves are not judged but they are by to hear,
> Although apparent guilt be seen in them;
> And shall the figure of God's majesty,
> His captain, steward, deputy elect,
> Anointed, crowned, planted many years,
> Be judged by subject and inferior breath,
> And he himself not present?
>
> (IV, i, 121–29)

He concludes with a prophecy of disaster:

> Disorder, horror, fear, and mutiny
> Shall here inhabit, and this land be called
> The field of Golgotha and dead men's skulls.
> O, if you raise this house against this house,
> It will the woefullest division prove
> That ever fell upon this cursed earth.
> Prevent it, resist it, let it not be so,
> Lest child, child's children cry against you
>     woe.
>
> (IV, i, 142–49)

Beyond this overt warning of future disaster, it is the devices by which the design of the play and its surface statement are reinforced and qualified that give this work its remarkable quality. It is a far cry from the simple chronicle with which Shakespeare started. It is not impeded in its impact by too much historical material, though it is not unfaithful to the truth of that material. Invention of various kinds is present on a scale that could not have been predicted from earlier history plays. The chronicle has suddenly become art.

A central image is that of the sun, iconographically equivalent to the king, its radiance obscured by clouds, eventually put into eclipse. Bolingbroke uses this image as Richard appears on the walls of Flint Castle:

> See, see, King Richard doth himself appear,
> As doth the blushing discontented sun
> From out the fiery portal of the east
> When he perceives the envious clouds are bent
> To dim his glory and to stain the track
> Of his bright passage to the occident.
>
> (III, iii, 62–67)

Richard modifies this image appropriately when he descends to the courtyard:

> Down, down I come, like glist'ring Phaeton,
> Wanting the manage of unruly jades.
>
> (III, iii, 178–79)

That is, by identifying with the son of Helios (the sun), who in trying to drive his father's golden chariot lost control of the horses, Richard can both describe his own disastrous downfall and admit his lack of skill in his divine role of king.

In IV, i, where the deposition is reenacted before Parliament, Richard uses a homelier image to describe his descent. He characterizes the handing over of the crown as being

> like a deep well
> That owes [has] two buckets, filling one
> another,
> The emptier ever dancing in the air,

> The other down, unseen, and full of water.
> That bucket down and full of tears am I,
> Drinking my griefs whilst you mount up on
>      high.
>
> (IV, i, 184–89)

He puts the two images together a few lines later:

> O that I were a mockery king of snow,
> Standing before the sun of Bolingbroke
> To melt myself away in water drops!
>
> (IV, i, 260–62)

Bolingbroke is now resplendent in kingship; Richard's tears are both for what he has lost and in recognition of the ephemeral nature of royal pomp and power.

These metaphorical flights are essentially descriptive and recapitulate Richard's fall without comment on its meaning. Therefore, between the descent at Flint Castle and the legal deposition in Parliament, a little symbolic scene is introduced. Two gardeners, commenting on affairs of state, liken Richard to a bad gardener, whose kingdom

> Is full of weeds, her fairest flowers choked up,
> Her fruit trees all unpruned, her hedges ruined,
> Her knots disordered, and her wholesome herbs
> Swarming with caterpillars . . .
>             . . . O, what pity is it
> That he had not so trimmed and dressed his
>      land
> As we this garden!
>
> (III, iv, 44–47, 55–57)

That is the case against Richard in down-to-earth terms. However painful it is, it is necessary that Bolingbroke come to pluck up the weeds "That seemed in eating him to hold him up" and to rid the kingdom of the parasitic infestation of the king's favorites.

But that is only half the story. The queen, grieving in the garden, steps forward and challenges the gardener:

> Thou old Adam's likeness, set to dress this
>    garden,
> How dares thy harsh rude tongue sound this
>    unpleasing news?
> What Eve, what serpent, hath suggested thee
> To make a second fall of cursed man?
>
> (III, iv, 73–76)

Ignoring the moral implications of the queen's question, the gardener stoutly holds to his practical point of view but takes up Richard's earlier metaphor in a new variation:

> Their fortunes both are weighed.
> In your lord's scale is nothing but himself,
> And some few vanities that make him light;
> But in the balance of great Bolingbroke,
> Besides himself, are all the English peers,
> And with that odds he weighs King Richard
>    down.
>
> (III, iv, 84–89)

Thus we see that there is a fatal gap between the immediate pragmatic advantage of restoring order to the garden by firing the gardener and the far-reaching consequences of that act. Deposing Richard is like the sin of Adam and the consequent expulsion from the Garden of Eden, and it will bring death into the world and endless woe.

The scene just discussed brings together the complex imagistic patterns that give the play its unique quality. Garden imagery is pervasive from the beginning, being especially evident in John of Gaunt's dying speech (II, i, 31 ff), where he too characterizes England as "This other Eden" and sees Richard treating the kingdom as oppressive landlord, not as benevolent king. From the beginning also, there is a continual play on the idea of tongue-flattery-serpent, which in effect recapitulates the snare set in Eden by the devil. That is to say, in immediate terms, that Richard has been seduced from his proper function by the blandishments of sycophants whose intentions are evil.

Another and equally important image strand has to do with blood. The Dowager Duchess of Gloucester speaks of King Edward's sons as

> seven vials of sacred blood,
> Or seven fair branches springing from one root,
> (I, ii, 12–13)

thus tying the blood imagery in with the garden imagery. It is the spilling of her husband's sacred blood that has provoked the immediate crisis confronting the kingdom. Yet that crisis will only be compounded by the spilling of Richard's blood, as we are warned by the Bishop of Carlisle:

> let me prophesy,
> The blood of English shall manure the ground
> And future ages groan for this foul act.
> (IV, i, 136–38)

Rather than fight, Richard has the wisdom to dismiss what is left of his army

> To ear [plow] the land that hath some hope to grow.
> (III, ii, 212)

Bolingbroke denies that it is his intention that

> such crimson tempest should bedrench
> The fresh green lap of fair King Richard's land.
> (III, iii, 46–47)

Richard counters that his cousin has come with war-like purpose and will

> bedew
> Her pastor's grass with faithful English blood.
> (III, iii, 99–100)

And the play ends with Bolingbroke, sobered by Richard's murder, lamenting

> That blood should sprinkle me to make me
> grow.
> (V, vi, 46)

In short, a whole pattern of images—much more complex than what has just been described—works to direct attention to the meaning of the events that the audience is witnessing. Granting that poetic subtleties of this nature are best followed in reading a text, it cannot be denied that by reiteration these images do lodge in the spectator's mind and do condition his response to the play. We here encounter a fourth unity, one whose cohesive force is at least equal to that of the unities of time, place, and action.

Not only does this imagistic unity control *Richard II*, it extends forward, conceptually at least, to the plays that follow it. Henry IV, in the plays that bear his name, never forgets the doubtful legality of his kingship. Henry V's successes grow out of his father's advice to quiet conflict at home by waging war abroad, but the disasters that follow his premature death derive directly from the breaking of the legitimate line by the removal of Richard II. This play, then, is both an examination of the moral right of deposition and a proem to a larger drama about the fate of the usurping Lancastrian kings.

Of all Shakespeare's history plays this is the one that caused the most contemporary excitement. Three quarto editions appeared in rapid succession. A contemporary record asserts that "This tragedy was played forty times in open streets and houses." On February 7, 1601, supporters of the Earl of Essex paid for a performance at the Globe Theater that put on the forbidden deposition scene (IV, i) in the hope of stirring up popular enthusiasm for the Earl of Essex's attempt to seize the throne. The coup d'état fell flat. Essex was executed. There is no record of punishment handed out to Shakespeare and the members of his company, though they may well have received some sort of royal rebuke. In any event, it was only after Elizabeth's death that it was safe to incorporate the deposition scene in acted and printed versions of the play.

## The First Part of
## King Henry the Fourth

This play (and its sequel) is only inciden-
tally about King Henry IV—the Bolingbroke of
*Richard II*. In general, the historical content is very
slight, being confined to the Percy rebellion of 1402–
03, which ended with the battle of Shrewsbury on
July 21, 1403.

Henry IV, looking forward to a condition of inter-
nal peace that will allow him to make his promised
pilgrimage to Jerusalem, is rudely shaken by two
threats to the kingdom's security. Owen Glendower, a
formidable Welsh guerrilla leader, has captured the
king's cousin, Sir Edmund Mortimer (on June 22,
1402), and a Scottish army has invaded the north of
England (September 14, 1402). However, in the latter
instance Henry Percy—"Hotspur"—has prevailed and
taken the Scottish Earl of Douglas captive. Hotspur
defies Henry IV by refusing to give up the captured
Douglas and by insisting that the king rescue Mortimer.* When the king will not recede from his position, Hotspur is eagerly and uncritically responsive to

---

* Shakespeare follows Holinshed's error in stating that Mortimer
is the heir to the throne in descent from Edward III's third son

the plans of his father, the Earl of Northumberland, and his uncle, the Earl of Worcester, to mount a rebellion in favor of Mortimer.

The Percy family, who had been Henry IV's chief supporters in the usurpation of 1399, feel that they have been slighted by the new king and foresee that he will attempt to reduce their powerful position. Accordingly they league together with the Earl of Douglas and with Glendower, whose daughter Edmund Mortimer has married. In spite of Hotspur's military valor, Henry IV proves the better strategist and quells the rebellion at Shrewsbury. Part of the reason for the defeat is Northumberland's decision not to commit his forces to battle. Worcester takes the crafty course of not informing Hotspur of the king's fair offer of compromise. Thus the battle is joined and Hotspur, the flower of English chivalry, is killed by Prince Hal, the Prince of Wales. The Earl of Worcester and Sir Richard Vernon are put to death two days later. The Earl of Douglas is set free in a gesture of magnanimity by the prince.

This historical action is only half the play. Balancing it is a purely fictional sequence involving riffraff elements from Eastcheap, a London slum. The dominant figure in this group is Sir John Falstaff, a member of the ruling class who has allowed himself to sink to a level of parasitical self-indulgence. Around him is a varied group: Poins, a gentleman's younger son; Bardolph, Peto, and Gadshill, ruffians and scroungers in varying degree; and Mistress Quickly, the hostess of a tavern.

When this group first appears, they are plotting the

---

Lionel. In fact, the heir is Mortimer's nephew, a boy of eleven, whom Richard II before his death had designated as his heir. Henry IV had that member of the Mortimer family safely in custody at Windsor Castle.

holdup of a king's messenger with the connivance of the Prince of Wales himself. They do carry out the robbery, but for the most part their scenes are a zestful exhibition of London low life, with Falstaff simultaneously functioning as leader and butt of the comic action. Though there is no historical evidence for it, by Shakespeare's day there was a longstanding tradition of Prince Hal's profligate youth, from which he emerged to become the very model of a Christian king. This idea of the prodigal prince was already embodied in Shakespeare's source play, *The Famous Victories of Henry V*. It is fundamental to both parts of *Henry IV* and is referred to in *Henry V*.

The historical action and the comic action converge to form a series of contrasts of personalities and values in which Prince Hal is the central figure. The configuration of the play is clear: Hal stands in the middle between Hotspur and Falstaff, sharing the virtues of both, repudiating the excesses of both, and achieving the middle ground of moderation based on self-knowledge. He shows that he will prove right royal when he ascends the throne. However, conclusive proof of his worthiness and the assumption of the throne itself are deferred to permit the development of a second play on much the same pattern of contrast.

The difficulty with many productions is that they do not give Hal sufficient stature. He is dwarfed by the brilliance of the other two major figures. In absentia, he seems to be merely the stimulus to many of Hotspur's outbursts of pride and on stage to be no more than the occasion for Falstaff's wit. Accordingly all too often the role is played by some engaging but undistinguished juvenile. Yet the play falls apart if Hal is allowed to be a cipher. Historically, to be sure, he was only sixteen at the battle of Shrewsbury, but in the play he must have dignity, maturity, and independent judgment.

Whatever the stature and attention due to Hal, it is true that he is not the center of the audience's interest. That is equally divided between Hotspur and Falstaff. Readers may overlook the equality of emphasis; spectators cannot, if the play is properly produced. They should be agog as to what each of these two characters will be up to next, dividing their attention between the two in a kind of seesaw. The correspondences of this balance are numerous, beginning with the fact that each man appears in seven scenes and culminating in the irony that the unvalorous Falstaff claims to have slain the valorous Hotspur. More significant is the fact that both are shown to be out of bounds in their behavior. Therefore both are dangerous to the realm and are potential misleaders of youth. They are the Scylla and Charybdis between which Hal must steer his course in this period of initiation.

Hotspur has a special importance because he is the paragon of knightly valor against whom Henry IV is constantly measuring his son. (The actual Hotspur was of the same generation as the king. But no matter. For the purposes of this play he must be coeval with Hal.) Singleminded in pursuit of glory, Hotspur is by no means monolithic in delineation. His every word and action moves the play forward. The scenes in which he appears are the high point of dramatic economy achieved by Shakespeare up to this time. By their perfection they are worthy of comparison with the mature achievement of Molière in such a play as *Tartuffe*.

Preparation for the appearance of Hotspur on stage comes with the king's opinion of him stated in the opening scene. Henry IV wishes his son were more like Hotspur but at the same time is disturbed by a recalcitrant streak in Hotspur's nature, which he ascribes to Northumberland's hostile influence. Two scenes later the king confronts the Percy faction in an angry mood. Hotspur's speech of self-justification (forty-one lines long) is remarkable for its vigor and homely idiom. It shows the impatience of his nature but also his saving sense of humor, as he parodies the perfumed lords who ordered him, still reeking of battle, to hand over his prisoners. When the king renews his demand for the prisoners and coldly leaves the room, Hotspur storms:

> An if the devil come and roar for them,
> I will not send them. I will after straight
> And tell him so; for I will ease my heart,
> Albeit I make a hazard of my head.
>
> (I, iii, 125–28)

To which Northumberland's reply: "What, drunk with choler?" is the pertinent commentary. The remainder of the scene between father, son, and uncle further exhibits Hotspur's intensity of reaction and headlong wilfulness. Thus when his elders confide that a plot against the king is in preparation, he enthusiastically and without analyzing the situation leaps to passionate adherence:

> I smell it. Upon my life, it will do well.
>
> (I, iii, 274)

While all of Hotspur is summed up in this scene, we are not allowed to get too simplified an impression. He shows unexpected tenderness when he takes leave of his wife. In the scene in which he and the other leaders of the rebellion prematurely divide up the kingdom, we see a playful side to him as he taunts Glendower almost beyond endurance. Though Hotspur flies off the handle easily, especially when confronted with pretentious fools, he is aware of what he is doing and in fact enjoys the risks incurred through his own excess. He is not stupid, nor is his sensitivity completely dulled by his career as fighting man. Yet he is constitutionally unable to heed the pauser reason and so becomes the dupe of duller but more calculating minds. His gallantry, wit, and singleminded devotion to the cause of honor do not prevent his being reduced to the level of pawn on the board of power politics, to be ruthlessly sacrificed by those black rooks, his father and uncle. That sacrifice occurs at the battle of Shrewsbury when his elders do not inform him of the king's offer of conciliation. Instead they are willing to send his inadequate forces into battle as a test of strength, while they reserve the better part of their own armies so as to be able to fight another day if Hotspur fails.

Falstaff is an even more remarkable creation than Hotspur. He is at first glance one of those characters whose excesses it is the function of comedy to correct —like Sir Toby Belch in *Twelfth Night*. Certainly comic deflation is continuously present in the scenes in which Falstaff appears, but the correction does not take place. By his wit, by his resilience, by his overwhelming vitality, he turns the tables on his would-be correctors time after time and bounces back unabashed from the humiliations they have set for him. He is a far cry from the mechanical buffoon of *The Merry Wives of Windsor*.

Hal and his companion Poins, while appearing to go along with the robbery of the king's messenger, actually arrange to set upon Falstaff and the other robbers and to rob and put them to flight. When Falstaff reappears he tells a wildly exaggerated story of courageous resistance. Hal thinks that he has Falstaff cornered, but the latter escapes his humiliation by exclaiming:

> By the Lord, I knew ye as well as he that made
> ye. . . . Was it for me to kill the heir apparent?
> Should I turn upon the true prince? Why, thou
> knowest I am as valiant as Hercules, but beware
> instinct. The lion will not touch the true prince.
>
> (II, iv, 253–57)

His statement is so open, so infectiously goodnatured,
that he almost convinces us that he did know all the
time.

When Falstaff and Hal pretend that they are king
and prince in a serious conversation about Hal's mis-
behavior, and Hal verbally anatomizes him as the
rogue he is, Falstaff is able to come back with a defense against Hal's catalogue of faults that is completely disarming:

> . . . but for sweet Jack Falstaff, kind Jack Falstaff,
> true Jack Falstaff, valiant Jack Falstaff, and there-
> fore more valiant being, as he is, old Jack Falstaff,
> banish not him thy Harry's company, banish not
> him thy Harry's company. Banish plump Jack, and
> banish all the world!
>
> (II, iv, 451–56)

Hal's "I do, I will!" in answer is a warning that goes
unnoticed as the spectators accept Falstaff's identifica-
tion with themselves, that is, with common humanity.
Immediately capping this exchange, when the sheriff
comes to inquire about the robbery, Hal and Peto
discover the knight sleeping unperturbed behind the
arras, the very picture of innocence.

In a later scene in which Falstaff fulminates about
having had his pocket picked of a sum such as he has
never been known to have, and receives from Mistress
Quickly the retort that he not only had nothing worth
stealing but is a notorious liar—claiming, for example,

that the prince owes him a thousand pounds—Falstaff adroitly retrieves himself in the prince's presence: "Thy love is worth a million; thou owest me thy love" (III, iii, 130–31). When he realizes that his outrageous boast of having killed Hotspur on the battlefield will not be credited, he backs down with quick improvisation:

> If I may be believed, so; if not, let them that should reward valor bear the sin upon their own heads. I'll take it upon my death, I gave him this wound in the thigh [administered after death].
>
> (V, iv, 145–50)

A halfpennyworth of truth to an intolerable deal of lying.

The visual and auditory facts of the matter are that Falstaff is a glutton, a liar, and a completely self-regarding man. He does rob the king's messenger; he is physically gross; he is a coward; he is insensitive to the feelings and well-being of others. Yet for the time being, none of this evidence greatly lowers him in our estimation. This is partly because of his defensive self-deprecation. He makes fun of his own girth. He ironically justifies his own cowardice. Better a live dog than a dead lion, we conclude along with him, as we see Hotspur lying dead. Early in the play he has set out for the robbery with the rallying cry, "They hate us youth." His implication is that the establishment is sterile and life-denying and that he, for all his white hairs, is young and on the side of life. It is of this vitality that Hal is thinking when at Shrewsbury he is under the impression that Falstaff is dead:

> I could have better spared a better man.
> O, I should have a heavy miss of thee

If I were much in love with vanity.

(V, iv, 103–05)

There are explicit warnings throughout the play that we must not accept Falstaff unreservedly. After the first Eastcheap scene, Hal lets us know in soliloquy how he feels about his apparently boon companions:

> I know you all, and will awhile uphold
> The unyoked humor of your idleness.
> Yet herein will I imitate the sun,
> Who doth permit the base contagious clouds
> To smother up his beauty from the world,
> That, when he please again to be himself,
> Being wanted, he may be more wond'red at
> By breaking through the foul and ugly mists
> Of vapors that did seem to strangle him.
>
> (I, ii, 183–91)

Falstaff himself, referring to more than his massive belly, asserts, "I live out of all order, out of all compass" (III, iii, 17). This is forcefully echoed by Sir Walter Blunt's rebuke to Hotspur at Shrewsbury that the latter is "out of limit and true rule," thereby bracketing the attitudes of Falstaff and Hotspur together as subversive of social order. In spite of these warnings Falstaff remains almost unscathed in our estimation. The symmetry of the play is therefore not complete. Hotspur is dead and discredited, but the fat knight lives on uncorrected and unrepentant.

Quite aside from the enjoyment that Falstaff's buffooneries on stage provide, he stands for a kind of freedom that all men desire and few have the courage to achieve. No one has stated this so well as A. C. Bradley:

> Falstaff's ease and enjoyment are not simply those of the happy man of appetite; they are those of the

humorist, and the humorist of genius. Instead of being comic to you and serious to himself, he is more ludicrous to himself than to you; and he makes himself out more ludicrous than he is, in order that he and others may laugh. . . .

The bliss of freedom gained in humour is the essence of Falstaff. His humour is not directed only or chiefly against obvious absurdities; he is the enemy of everything that would interfere with his ease, and therefore of anything serious, and especially of everything respectable and moral. For these things impose limits and obligations, and make us the subjects of old father antic the law. . . . They are to him absurd; and to reduce a thing *ad absurdum* is to reduce it to nothing and to walk about free and rejoicing.

That freedom, however, must ultimately be weighed in the balance. As so often happens, it is the good sense of Dr. Samuel Johnson that gives us the proper perspective:

But Falstaff, unimitated, unimitable Falstaff, how shall I describe thee! thou compound of sense and vice; of sense which may be admired, but not esteemed; of vice that may be despised, but hardly detested. Falstaff is a character loaded with faults, and with those faults which naturally produce contempt. . . . It must be observed, that he is stained with no enormous or sanguinary crimes, so that his licentiousness is not so offensive but that it may be borne for his mirth.

The moral to be drawn from this representation is, that no man is more dangerous than he that, with a will to corrupt, hath the power to please; and that neither wit nor honesty ought to think themselves safe with such a companion, when they see Henry seduced by Falstaff.

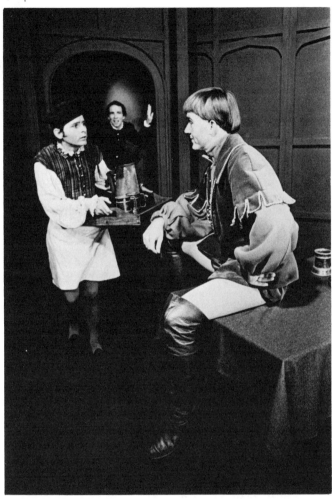

Prince Hal (Tom Donaldson), seated right, and Poins (Richard Allan Edwards), in the doorway, tease Francis the waiter (Gregory Ward Schroeder) in *1 Henry IV*.

RIGHT: Falstaff (Garry Moore) drives out blustering Pistol (Richard Riehle) in the presence of Doll Tearsheet (Alice Rorvik), left, and Mistress Quickly (Diana Bellamy), right, in *2 Henry IV*.

BOTH PHOTOS: CAROLYN MASON JONES.

OREGON SHAKESPEAREAN FESTIVAL, ASHLAND, OREGON.

Prince Hal (Alan Howard), newly crowned as Henry V, rejects Falstaff (Brewster Mason) and tells him to amend his ways in *2 Henry IV*. Supporting figures, left to right, are Westmoreland (Reginald Jessup), Clarence (Anthony Naylor), Gloucester (Stephen Jenn), Lancaster (Charles Dance), Lord Chief Justice (Griffith Jones), Davy (Philip Braek), Silence (Trevor Peacock), Bardolph (Tom Wylton), and Pistol (Richard Moore).

BY KIND PERMISSION OF THE ROYAL SHAKESPEARE THEATRE, STRATFORD-UPON-AVON.

King Henry V (Laurence Olivier) woos Princess Katherine of France (Renée Asherson) in the presence of her chaperone Alice (Ivy St. Helier) in the film version of *Henry V*, V, ii. The setting for this scene is modeled after illustrations in a medieval *Book of the Hours*.

BY PERMISSION OF THE MUSEUM OF MODERN ART, FILM STILLS ARCHIVE.

The Dauphin, later Charles VII of France (Gail Chugg), kneels in gratitude before Joan la Pucelle (Elisabeth Keller), who has raised the siege of Orléans, in *1 Henry VI*.

LEFT: Fluellen (James Smith) humiliates Pistol (Charles G. Taylor) in a scene from *Henry V*: "I pray you, fall to: If you can mock a leek, you can eat a leek."

BOTH PHOTOS: DWAINE SMITH.

OREGON SHAKESPEAREAN FESTIVAL, ASHLAND, OREGON.

Richard III (Ian Richardson), having usurped the throne,
spurns Buckingham (Tony Church), who has been a principal supporter in that enterprise.
BY KIND PERMISSION OF THE ROYAL SHAKESPEARE THEATER,
STRATFORD-UPON-AVON.

King Richard III (Laurence Olivier) leads his unwilling
queen, Anne (Claire Bloom), to her coronation in a scene
interpolated in the film version of *Richard III*.
BY PERMISSION OF THE MUSEUM OF MODERN ART,
FILM STILLS ARCHIVE.

Dr. Johnson here touches on a theme that binds the play together—the falsity of appearances, an essential ambiguity of persons and events. This duplicity pervades the entire tetralogy as far as public events are concerned. An usurpation that promises stability brings insurrection, as supporters of the king soon find it tempting to unseat him. Both parts of *Henry IV* are built on this. And as the tetralogy ends with the triumph of King Henry V, who was once the delinquent Prince Hal, the audience knows—and is reminded by the epilogue—that all this glory is illusion, to become dust and ashes in the reign of Henry VI.

It is in *1 Henry IV* that this playing with appearance/reality is most varied and most sustained. Prince Hal is not what he seems; he tells us so at the first opportunity. The king, Hotspur, and Falstaff all misread him. The king sees "riot and dishonor stain his brow," and fears that God is using his son as "revengement and a scourge for me." Hotspur accepts the common opinion of Hal, on the battlefield condescendingly wishing to God that

> Thy name in arms were now as great as mine!

Falstaff sees Hal as malleable clay. It tickles his vanity to have the king's son as companion and foil, but there is calculation as well. He imagines himself in the role of surrogate father to the next king, a fantasy that he acts out in II, iv, 358 ff.

False appearances underlie the action of the play. Hal and Poins stage a fake holdup of Falstaff. Glendower deludes himself with the idea that he has supernatural powers, a pretension that Hotspur gleefully deflates. The conspirators misread the king's resolution and are suspicious of his offer of conciliation. Northumberland feigns sickness and leaves his son in the lurch at Shrewsbury. The latter, blinded by a vision of glory, makes a bad military decision and loses the battle. Finally, on the battlefield Henry IV sends out doubles dressed in his armor in order to delude and disperse his enemies. Falstaff counterfeits death, then counterfeits honor. Hotspur's honor is illusory if not counterfeit. Only Hal is not taken in by appearances. That is, indeed, the purpose of his education, to fit him to see life clearly and to see it whole.

A notable development of craftsmanship present in this play is the assurance with which high and low life, the serious and the comic, are welded together. This mixture of genres, forbidden by classical rules, became a hallmark of Shakespeare's dramaturgy. Nowhere in the canon is it so skillfully handled or so dramatically apposite as here, unless it be in *Twelfth Night*, where, after all, the issues are less serious. And nowhere does Shakespeare provide as extended a presentation of what amounts to contemporary London life as in the two parts of *Henry IV*. This mixing of genres permits a new kind of spectacle, that of familiar, everyday life with its own peculiar usages, its vocabulary, and its characteristic human products.

Actually the gamut of low-life characters is restricted, and their activities are fairly innocent, if we can accept Hal's announced intention to pay back the money taken in the robbery as somehow palliating the offense. Much of the action is delightful and inconsequential horseplay. For example, in II, iv, Hal and Poins set up a farcical scene in which they simultaneously summon Francis, a dim-witted waiter, from two different rooms. Francis is practically torn apart as he attempts to respond to their calls. The increasingly frantic "Anon, anon, sir" with which he replies to each of them is the kind of catch phrase that becomes as obsessive as a popular tune. We can imagine all

London responding for a time to daily vexations with "Anon, anon, sir" until the craze is replaced by something else.

After Falstaff, the most individualized of the low-life characters are Bardolph and Mistress Quickly, he by reason of his red-veined toper's nose, she by her sentimental, credulous cast of mind at variance with her vocation of hard-bitten tavernkeeper. Because these figures were fresh and spoke in a language both authentic and individual, it is not surprising that they received further development in the two succeeding plays.

## The Second Part of King Henry the Fourth

This second play covering the reign of King Henry IV has two reasons for its existence. It gives audiences a chance for a further romp with inimitable Falstaff, whose popularity on the stage has never flagged since Shakespeare created him. And the play works toward and concludes with the great dramatic transformation by which Hal, the prodigal prince, becomes a hero-king.

The historical substance is slight and, to a degree, repetitive of the preceding play, from which it continues without a break. News of the disastrous outcome of the battle of Shrewsbury reaches the Earl of Northumberland. His grief over the death of his son Hotspur is excessive, when we consider his failure to provide military help for his son. He talks of revenging Hotspur's death, but is easily dissuaded by Hotspur's widow, who thinks pursuit of honor has taken sufficient toll. He then cautiously and characteristically decides to seek safety in Scotland.

Time is telescoped so that a new conspiracy, headed by the Archbishop of York and Thomas Mowbray (which took place in May–June 1405), seems to follow immediately. The conspirators demand redress of grievances and the removal of Henry IV in favor of Edmund Mortimer, whom they consider the legitimate heir, since he is descended from Edward III's third son. The rebellion receives wide support in the north—Percy country—and because of the archbishop's saintly reputation seems to be a hallowed cause. Holinshed said of him:

> Indeed, the respect that men had to the archbishop caused them to like the better of the cause, since the gravity of his age, his integrity of life, and incomparable learning, with the reverend aspect of his amiable personage, moved all men to have him in no small estimation.

King Henry and Hal are not involved in the military confrontation that takes place in Gaultree Forest. The leaders of the king's army are his younger son, Prince John, and the Earl of Westmoreland. The prince promises redress of the rebels' grievances and suggests the discharge of the soldiers on both sides. The rebel army is immediately dispersed; the king's is not. John arrests the rebel leaders and sends them off to execution. When accused of breaking faith, he denies that he has done so:

> I pawned thee none.
> I promised you redress of these same grievances
> Whereof you did complain, which, by mine honor,
> I will perform with a most Christian care.
> But for you, rebels, look to taste the due
> Meet for rebellion and such acts as yours. . . .
> God, and not we, hath safely fought to-day.
> Some guard these traitors to the block of death,
> Treason's true bed and yielder up of breath.
>                           (IV, ii, 112–23)

This whole sequence is perfunctory. Without Hotspur there is little to command audience attention. However, rebellion in high places continues to serve as a balance to Falstaff's subversion on a low level, and the cold-blooded calculation of Prince John by contrast adds to Hal's stature. Also the conspiracy is a continuing reminder of Henry IV's insecure hold on the crown he has usurped.

Without evident transition, the play leaps to Henry IV's fatal illness and death. Three scenes of high drama conclude the play. In IV, iv, Henry IV, recognizing that his life is coming to a close, fears for the future when Hal is king:

> Most subject is the fattest soil to weeds,
> And he, the noble image of my youth,
> Is overspread with them. Therefore my grief
> Stretches itself beyond the hour of death.
> The blood weeps from my heart when I do
>      shape
> In forms imaginary the unguided days
> And rotten times that you shall look upon
> When I am sleeping with my ancestors.
>
> (IV, iv, 54–61)

The Earl of Warwick attempts to allay this anxiety by asserting that the prince will profit from his experiences with the common people.

In the following scene, Hal appears and decides to sit by the king, who has fallen asleep with the crown on a pillow by his side. The prince meditates upon the burdens of kingship, puts on the crown, and walks away with it. The king, awakening, immediately puts the worst construction on Hal's action:

> How quickly nature falls into revolt
> When gold becomes her object!
>
> (IV, v, 65–66)

Hal reappears and exclaims:

> I never thought to hear you speak again.
> (IV, v, 91)

To which the king replies:

> Thy wish was father, Harry, to that thought.
> (IV, v, 92)

In a long diatribe, the king describes what the kingdom will be like under Hal:

> For now a time is come to mock at form.
> Harry the Fifth is crowned. Up, vanity!
> Down, royal State! . . .
> For the fifth Harry from curbed license plucks
> The muzzle of restraint, and the wild dog
> Shall flesh his tooth on every innocent.
> O my poor kingdom, sick with civil blows!
> When that my care could not withhold thy
> riots,
> What wilt thou do when riot is thy care?
> O, thou wilt be a wilderness again,
> Peopled with wolves, thy old inhabitants.
> (IV, v, 118–37)

Hal defends himself with dignity and humility. The king is satisfied:

> God put it in thy mind to take it [the crown]
> hence,
> That thou mightst win the more thy father's
> love,
> Pleading so wisely in excuse of it!
> (IV, v, 178–80)

Henry IV then admits that he has come to the crown by "bypaths and indirect crooked ways" and hopes that his son's claim will appear less tarnished. Always the realist, he suggests to Hal that he "busy giddy minds with foreign quarrels," thereby stifling dissent at home.

With Henry IV dead, trepidation as well as grief settles on the court. With instant sensitivity Hal detects and removes this · fear in the first of his fine speeches as king:

> This new and gorgeous garment, majesty,
> Sits not so easy on me as you think.
> Brothers, you mix your sadness with some fear.
> This is the English, not the Turkish court.
> Not Amurath an Amurath succeeds,
> But Harry Harry.
>
> (V, ii, 44–49)

Then Hal turns to the Lord Chief Justice, asking how the Chief Justice's act of sending Hal to prison for breaking the peace (part of the legend of the prodigal prince) can "be washed in Lethe, and forgotten?" The Chief Justice stoutly upholds the sanctity of the law and its supremacy over any individual, even the king's son. Hal's answer is gravely regal:

> Therefore still bear the balance and the sword.
> And I do wish your honors may increase,
> Till you do live to see a son of mine
> Offend you and obey you, as I did.
>
> (V, ii, 103–06)

The scene toward which both parts of *Henry IV* have been moving is that in which Falstaff is rejected, final proof of Hal's regeneration. As the new king comes from his coronation, Falstaff and his followers, eager for plunder and preferment, crowd around him. Hal first attempts to ignore the familiarity of his former friends, then unequivocally rejects Falstaff:

> I know thee not, old man. Fall to thy prayers.
> How ill white hairs become a fool and jester!
> I have long dreamed of such a kind of man,
> So surfeit-swelled, so old, and so profane,
> But, being awaked, I do despise my dream.
> Make less thy body hence, and more thy grace.
> Leave gormandizing. Know the grave doth
>           gape
> For thee thrice wider than for other men.
> Reply not to me with a fool-born jest.
> Presume not that I am the thing I was,
> For God doth know, so shall the world
>           perceive,
> That I have turned away my former self.
> So will I those that kept me company.
> When thou dost hear I am as I have been,
> Approach me, and thou shalt be as thou wast,
> The tutor and the feeder of my riots.
>
> (V, v, 48–63)

No episode in all of Shakespeare has aroused more protest than this rejection of Falstaff, unless it be Hamlet's treatment of Ophelia or the punishment meted out to Shylock. Whatever one's judgment of the king, Falstaff's end is in his beginning, or rather in Hal's :

> I know you all, and will awhile uphold
> The unyoked humor of your idleness.
>
> (*1 Henry IV*, I, ii, 183–84)

Hal then promises a reformation so dazzling that men will forget his fault because he will redeem time "when men least think I will." This change in behavior is a necessary part of the legend of the prodigal prince. Holinshed refers to it—without reference to the fictional Falstaff—when he says of Hal:

. . . he determined to put on him the shape of a
new man. For whereas aforetime he had made himself a companion unto misruly mates of dissolute
order and life, he now banished them all from his
presence (but not unrewarded, or else unpre-
ferred); inhibiting them upon a great pain, not
once to approach, lodge, or sojourn within ten
miles of his court or presence.

Falstaff, however, takes such hold on the affections
of the spectator that it is not easy to make rejection
palatable. To that end, in *2 Henry IV*, Shakespeare attempts to diminish the attractiveness of the fat knight.
First of all, there is minimal contact with Hal. The two
appear together on stage only once before the final
scene. This occurs in II, iv, in a colloquy of less than
100 lines, in which Hal is condescending, almost abu-
sive, and Falstaff is obsequious, almost abject. The exchange breaks off suddenly when both are summoned
to court. Falstaff delays answering the call of duty as
usual; Hal leaves forthwith, expressing guilt "So idly
to profane the precious time," and disappears from
Eastcheap forever.

Another way in which Falstaff is demeaned is by the
introduction of new and unsavory characters, or by
the addition of unsavory traits to his old companions.
The trim minuscule page with whom Hal has slyly
endowed Falstaff is a constant reproach to the knight's
great girth and general sloppiness. Pistol, a very braggart soldier, is a brand new character whose bombastic
utterance does not conceal his self-seeking and preda-
tory nature. Doll Tearsheet, a whore, is another addition to this questionable group. Even Mistress Quickly
is downgraded. She has received the unfavorable notice of the police for running a disorderly establishment. By brilliant extension of Falstaff's happy hunt-
ing grounds, Shakespeare takes him to Gloucestershire

for three scenes—to the sticks, we would say, since Gloucestershire, a county lying far to the west, on the Welsh border, is completely outside the Londoner's experience. Its rustics, however, are easily recognizable as rascals by the knowing city dweller's eye.

Each of the six scenes in which Falstaff appears before the rejection contains either an outright rebuke or a demonstration of his least pleasant characteristics. His first encounter (I, ii) is with the Lord Chief Justice, who is most improbably walking the streets of Eastcheap, a London slum. The scene is notable for Falstaff's impudence, which he carries so far as to try to borrow a thousand pounds from the justice. Neither party in the encounter comes off well. The justice is baffled by Falstaff; Falstaff's wit is unable to surmount the justice's criticism, which boils down to advice that the knight act his age and mend his ways.

The justice again appears, fortuitously, in II, i, where Falstaff is being arrested for debt by long-suffering Mistress Quickly. When Falstaff attempts to weasel out of his difficulties by calling her "a poor mad soul" who "says up and down the town that her eldest son is like" the justice, the latter makes a pointed rebuke: "I am well acquainted with your manner of wrenching the true cause the false way." Mistress Quickly, a born gull, relents in her suit and is willing to accommodate Falstaff by selling her silverware. Falstaff clowns a bit in relief, and the scene ends with the justice calling him "a great fool."

Not only does Prince Hal show indifference toward Falstaff in II, iv, but the knight becomes grotesque in his lovemaking with Doll Tearsheet. Even she perceives the incongruity of his lechery and says to him:

> Thou whoreson little tidy Bartholomew boar-pig, when wilt thou leave fighting o' days and foining

[copulating] o' nights, and begin to patch up thine old body for heaven?

(II, iv, 214–16)

However, the scene does end on a note of incongruous praise from the inconstant tongue of Mistress Quickly:

Well, fare thee well. I have known thee these twenty-nine years, come peascod-time, but an honester and truer-hearted man—well, fare thee well.

(II, iv, 358–60)

In Gloucestershire, Falstaff is received as a man of importance by his hosts, Justices of the Peace Shallow and Silence. He shocks even them, experienced as they are in minor skulduggery, by his choice of recruits for the king's army. Instead of selecting the most likely soldiers, Falstaff lets them off— in return for a bribe— and chooses scarecrows whose only virtue is that they might frighten the enemy. He abuses the authority that he has under the king, and he violates humanity by his unconcern for the men whose lives he holds in balance.

Smelling out fat pickings among these rustics, Falstaff arranges a return to Gloucestershire in V, i. Falstaff feels himself far superior to these country bumpkins and observes that he "will devise matter enough out of this Shallow to keep Prince Harry in continual laughter." As he lingers with the justices, eating and drinking at their expense, word comes of the death of Henry IV. Falstaff is immediately in an ecstasy of expectation. He says to his host:

Master Shallow, my Lord Shallow—be what thou wilt, I am fortune's steward—get on thy boots.

We'll ride all night. . . . I know the young king is
sick for me. Let us take any man's horses; the laws
of England are at my commandment. Blessed are
they that have been my friends, and woe to my
lord chief justice!

(V, iii, 126–35)

And Shallow willingly lends Falstaff a thousand
pounds.

The rejection by the new king takes place in the
presence of Shallow. Falstaff is for a moment shocked
into recognition of his true situation, turning to the
country justice with the honest admission: "Master
Shallow, I owe you a thousand pound." Then Falstaff
seeks refuge in illusion again, observing: "Look you,
he must seem thus to the world. Fear not your ad-
vancements; I will be the man yet that shall make you
great." Shallow is not taken in. He goes back to
Gloucestershire a poorer, but not necessarily wiser,
man.

On the face of it, the varied elements of which this
play is made—renewed rebellion in the north, the further adventures of Falstaff and company, and Prince
Hal's regeneration—have no unity. Beneath these disparate actions, however, there is a broad pattern of
images that provides a unifying framework of myth.
The kingdom is sick, and, as the play progresses, its
king is dying, morally as well as physically under-
mined by corruption. Indeed, the king must die, so
that Hal, who represents regenerative forces, a healing
power for the ailing commonwealth, may ascend the
throne.

Age, disease, and corruption are equated throughout
the play. At the very beginning, Rumor, busily dis-
seminating false information in the interest of public
disorder, characterizes "old" Northumberland as lying

"crafty–sick." The various conspiracies with which Henry IV has to deal are seen as a pervasive disease that is wasting away the commonwealth. The first rebellion was led by Hotspur, a young man, a leader of undoubted vitality and promise. Now the leaders are old and sunk in self-interest, whatever gloss of piety they may put on their intentions. Surprisingly, they seem to embrace a principle of anarchic violence. After Hotspur's death Northumberland exclaims:

> Let order die!
> And let this world no longer be a stage
> To feed contention in a lingering act.
> But let one spirit of the first-born Cain
> Reign in all bosoms, that, each heart being set
> On bloody courses, the rude scene may end,
> And darkness be the burier of the dead!
> (I, i, 154–60)

He does not, of course, commit himself to this vision of ultimate chaos, but the play asserts that it is what underlies the conventional and self-righteous utterances of the rebel leaders.

They harp on the violation to the realm brought about by Henry's usurpation—to which they gave their support. The land, they say, is bleeding with Richard II's blood. The Archbishop of York believes the kingdom is now sick of its own choice and ready to vomit up the usurping king. Henry IV himself on his first appearance picks up this disease imagery:

> Then you perceive the body of our kingdom
> How foul it is, what rank diseases grow,
> And with what danger, near the heart of it.
> (III, i, 37–40)

At the height of the rebellion (IV, i, 53 ff) the Archbishop of York echoes and extends the king's assessment:

> we are all diseased,
> And with our surfeiting and wanton hours
> Have brought ourselves into a burning fever,
> And we must bleed for it.

This is one focus of the imagistic statement. There is a deep-seated sickness in the kingdom, traceable to Henry's usurpation and the murder of Richard, that leads and will lead to rebellion after rebellion. At the same time this moral cancer in the king is accompanied by, and accounts for, the physical illness that leaves him languid, fearful, and incapable of rule—"a fangless lion."

The other part of the picture of age, disease, and corruption is more sustained and more detailed. The immediate target is Falstaff's claim to perpetual youth. Falstaff tells the Lord Chief Justice that "You that are old consider not the capacities of us that are young; you do measure the heat of our livers with the bitterness of your galls" (I, ii, 165–68). Quite properly the justice denies this claim to youth with vigor:

> Do you set down your name in the scroll of youth,
> that are written down old with all the characters
> of age? Have you not a moist eye? A dry hand?
> A yellow cheek? A white beard? A decreasing leg?
> An increasing belly? Is not your voice broken?
> Your wind short? Your chin double? Your wit
> single? And every part about you blasted with
> antiquity?
>
> (I, ii, 170–75)

The broad and often bawdy comedy of Falstaff's scene with Doll Tearsheet continues this emphasis on physical corruption. The fat knight's fondling of the whore and her honeyed responses are grotesque—a display that on Falstaff's part is a desperate counter-offensive against the encroachment of age. After Doll has suggested that he "begin to patch up thine old body for heaven," Falstaff begs her not to "speak like a death's-head. Do not bid me remember mine end" (II, iv, 217–18).

The first of the Gloucestershire scenes picks up the theme of age immediately, as Justices Shallow and Silence recall their days at the Inns of Court [law school] and lament that so many of their acquaintances are dead. Shallow's greeting to Falstaff is not one to give the latter pleasure:

> By my troth, you like [thrive] well and bear your years very well. Welcome, good Sir John.
>
> (III, ii, 80–81)

The justices cackle over youthful exploits that never happened and never could have happened. Again the refrain of "old, old" is uttered as they recall those they knew fifty-five years before.

The corruption of these old men appears in various ways. There is the impotent and grotesque lecherousness of Silence. There is the venality of Shallow, who bends the law in his own interest, just as Falstaff accepts bribes to excuse the best specimens among the recruits. The greed of the justices is parallel to Falstaff's own expectations when Hal becomes king. In all of them we see the potential expansion of tolerated venality to a level of public corruption that would bring down the kingdom and justify the worst fears of Henry IV and the Lord Chief Justice.

In contrast to the avarice, the calculation, and the posturing of these old men is the simple acceptance of

duty by young Feeble, one of the recruits whom Falstaff presses into service:

> A man can die but once. We owe God a death.
> I'll ne'er bear a base mind. An't be my destiny, so.
> An't be not, so. No man is too good to serve's
> prince. And let it go which way it will, he that
> dies this year is quit for the next.
>
> (III, ii, 221–25)

A timely reminder that there is sound and vital stock
that, given favorable conditions, will grow and flourish.

The emphasis on age and corruption on all levels,
however, produces a picture of a society declining
into death, painfully striving to hold itself together
but secretly fearing dissolution. Against this background Prince Hal stands out as a figure of hope. He
removes himself from the contagion of Falstaff, mocks
him in their one brief conversation, and at the end
rejects him in terms that underline the indecency of
corrupt age. Hal's role is to transcend corruption, to
reenact the age-old ritual of killing the sick and impotent king, and thereby to restore health to the kingdom. It is in this context that the taking away of his
father's crown assumes more than literal significance.
Not only does this act serve to introduce a moment of
suspense, as the audience wonders whether Hal is
firmly on the path of reformation, but it also stands as
a kind of symbolic slaying of the king.

Thus the end of the play has a threefold significance. The anticipated historical event—the accession
of Hal—takes place. The prince effects the reformation that he promised at the beginning of Part One.
And as healing and regenerative force, he wipes the

slate clean for the beginning of a golden age. As Henry IV tells his son,

> . . . all the soil of the achievement [his
>      usurpation] goes
> With me into the earth.

(IV, v, 189–90)

At least that is his hope. The spectator is no doubt aware of the irony underlying this expectation, the fact that so splendid a king as Henry V will reign only nine years and that all he will accomplish will fall in ruin. But this does not impair the jubilation that the end of the play brings.

# The Life of
# King Henry the Fifth

During the short and glorious reign of Henry V, the English achieved what they had long sought, the complete (though temporary) subjugation of France. The events covered by the play begin with the sending of a derisive gift of tennis balls by the Dauphin of France in the spring of 1414, a year after Henry's accession. The play ends with Henry's betrothal to Princess Katherine of France at Troyes in May 1420. The central action is the military expedition against France that culminated in the famous victory at Agincourt on October 25, 1415.

In August 1415, while preparing to launch an invasion from Southampton, Henry V became aware of a conspiracy headed by Richard Earl of Cambridge, who sought the crown for his cousin Mortimer (in expectation that after Mortimer's death it would come to him). After execution of the chief conspirators, the king and his forces disembarked near Harfleur on August 14. They besieged Harfleur, which did not yield until September 22. By the time the king left there on October 8, his army was riddled with sickness and winter was imminent. Therefore, Henry asked the French for safe conduct across the north of France to the English fortress city of Calais. The French refused, convinced that they could wipe out the English army. Holinshed states that the English force consisted of "only two thousand horsemen, and thirteen thousand archers, billmen, and of all sorts of other footmen," whereas the French force amounted to "three-score thousand horsemen, besides footmen, wagoners, and others."

Whatever the accuracy of these figures, the French boastfully caroused the night before the battle, while the English anticipated the dawn with dread. An emissary was even sent to ask Henry V what ransom he would offer after he was captured. (The Dauphin, who in the play is the most boastful among the French, was in fact not at the battle. Neither were the Earl of Westmoreland and the king's brother, John Duke of Bedford, whom Shakespeare has placed there.) In the battle, named after the castle of Agincourt nearby, the rout of the French was complete. Some ten thousand men were slain and at least fifteen hundred taken prisoner, including Charles Duke of Orléans, the French king's nephew. The English, again according to Holinshed, lost Edward Duke of York (the king's cousin), the Earl of Suffolk, and some five and twenty others.

Henry V crossed over to Dover with his prisoners on November 16 and received a festive welcome in London (described in the play by the Chorus to Act V). Shakespeare completely ignores a second and more serious military campaign begun on August 1, 1417, which caused the French to sue for peace and brought about the meeting at Troyes in May 1420 that is the substance of the last act. By the treaty signed there Henry V was betrothed to Katherine of France. (Negotiations for this marriage had been going on since 1415, and Henry had actually met her a year earlier.) It was also settled by treaty that Henry V would be regent of France during the remaining years of the French king's life, would be king of France thereafter, and that his and Katherine's son would be king of both countries. The Dauphin was thus disinherited.

Shakespeare's selection of historical materials, and the emphasis he gives them, is controlled by his central purpose: to give an heroic portrait of Henry V. In this he is following popular legend, especially Holinshed's almost reverent account of the king:

> This Henry was a king, of life without spot; a prince whom all men loved, and of none disdained; a captain against whom fortune never frowned, nor mischance once spurned; whose people him so severe a justicer both loved and obeyed, (and so humane withal,) that he left no offense unpunished, nor friendship unrewarded; a terror to rebels, and suppressor of sedition; his virtues notable, his qualities most praiseworthy. . . . Wantonness of life and thirst in avarice had he quite quenched in him. . . . For bountifulness and liberality, no man more free, gentle, and frank, in bestowing rewards to all persons, according to their deserts: for his saying was, that he never desired money to keep, but to give and spend. . . .
> . . . Known be it therefore, of person and form was this prince rightly representing his heroical affects; of stature and proportion tall and manly, rather lean than gross, somewhat long necked, and black haired, of countenance amiable; eloquent and grave was his speech, and of great grace and power to persuade; for conclusion, a majesty was he that that both lived & died a pattern in princehood, a lodestar in honor, and mirror of magnificence; the more highly exalted in his life, the more deeply

lamented at his death, and famous to the world always.

The first episodes of the play build up the character of the king. There is repeated reference to his profligate youth—by members of the court, by representatives of the church, by the French, and by his former companions in Eastcheap—as a contrast to his present kingly grace. This praise is particularly fulsome from the Archbishop of Canterbury, who characterizes Henry V as a kind of universal man (I, i, 39 ff).

More important in establishing his greatness are his bearing, words, and actions. He is impressive for his disciplined attitude. He is not rash. Before embarking on his expedition to France, Henry receives a thorough briefing as to his rights to the French crown from the Archbishop of Canterbury. The directness of the king's mind is in pleasant contrast with Canterbury's prolixity. Henry V shows becoming dignity when he receives the insulting gift of tennis balls from the Dauphin with the overt charge that Henry is only a playboy king. Henry's reply is one of measured menace:

> We are glad the Dauphin is so pleasant with
>     us . . .
> We will in France, by God's grace, play a set
> Shall strike his father's crown into the
>     hazard . . .
> And tell the pleasant prince this mock of his
> Hath turned his balls to gunstones, and his soul
> Shall stand sore charged for the wasteful
>     vengeance
> That shall fly with them; for many a thousand
>     widows
> Shall this his mock mock out of their dear
>     husbands,

Mock mothers from their sons, mock castles
     down;
And some are yet ungotten and unborn
That shall have cause to curse the Dauphin's
     scorn.
                              (I, ii, 260 ff)

Underlying this speech and the one in which he
castigates the conspirators at Southampton (II, ii, 79
ff) is a moral certainty that sets Henry on a level
above common men. His words give evidence of
moral superiority, of passions that are impersonal, essentially royal, emanating not from resentment at the
affront to his person, but from concern for the well-
being of the kingdom. From godlike eminence Henry
looks down on and chides inferior beings for their
folly (in the case of the Dauphin) or for their crimi-
nality (in the case of the conspirators), both of which
are offences " 'gainst all proportion." With respect to
the conspirators there is a further charge. They are
men of breeding, responsibility, and apparent moral
sense; yet they have turned their nobility to baseness:

                         I will weep for thee;
     For this revolt of thine, methinks, is like
     Another fall of man. Their faults are open.
     Arrest them to the answer of the law;
     And God acquit them of their practices!
                              (II, ii, 140–44)

The basic strategy up to this point of the play is to
measure King Henry against those around him, to exhibit his kingly capacity by means of a series of dis-
continuous contrasts. The first is with the Archbishop
of Canterbury, more politician than saint, who en-
courages Henry's expedition to France in the hope
that a large voluntary contribution of money from the

church will avert a threatened confiscation of church lands. Henry's concern for the kingdom is in contrast with the self-seeking of the conspirators; his even-handed justice with their narrow partisanship. The French, as always in these plays, provide a ridiculous foil—effeminate, vainglorious, contemptible for their lack of seriousness, as is demonstrated in III, vii, on the eve of the battle of Agincourt.

At the center of the play is the exhibition of Henry V as valorous military leader, first, before Harfleur, then at the unsought battle. There are difficulties with this demonstration. The siege of Harfleur is successful, less by reason of English military prowess than by dereliction of the French. Moreover, it has been so prolonged that the invaders, facing sickness and the coming of winter, are forced to try to retreat to their permanent base at Calais. In other words, if we look at the situation closely, we find that the attributes of the king as a soldier—"a name that in my thoughts becomes me best," he says—have achieved very little. However, this is obscured by his rhetoric in battle and by the terrifying odds at Agincourt.

Two of Henry's exhortations to his troops are among the most often quoted patriotic poetry in the English language. As the soldiers attempt to scale the walls of besieged Harfleur in III, i, the king urges them on:

> Once more unto the breach, dear friends, once
> more,
> Or close the wall up with our English dead!
> In peace there's nothing so becomes a man
> As modest stillness and humility,
> But when the blast of war blows in our ears,
> Then imitate the action of the tiger: . . .
>                     And you, good yeoman,

> Whose limbs were made in England, show us
> here
> The mettle of your pasture. Let us swear
> That you are worth your breeding; which I
> doubt not,
> For there is none of you so mean and base
> That hath not noble lustre in your eyes.
> I see you stand like greyhounds in the slips,
> Straining upon the start. The game's afoot!
> Follow your spirit; and upon this charge
> Cry 'God for Harry! England and Saint
> George!'

Equally famous is the king's reply to the Earl of Westmoreland, who wishes there were with them at the battle of Agincourt ten thousand of those men in England who are idle:

> No, my fair cousin.
> If we are marked to die, we are enow
> To do our country loss; and if to live,
> The fewer men, the greater share of honor . . .
> From this day to the ending of the world,
> But we in it shall be remembered—
> We few, we happy few, we band of brothers;
> For he to-day that sheds his blood with me
> Shall be my brother. Be he ne'er so vile,
> This day shall gentle his condition;
> And gentlemen in England now abed
> Shall think themselves accursed they were not
> here,
> And hold their manhoods cheap whiles any
> speaks
> That fought with us upon Saint Crispin's day.
> (IV, iii, 19–22; 58–67)

The battle itself is a crisis situation in which King Henry demonstrates his humility and self-abnegation, his paternal care for his subjects, and also examines his own conscience as he meditates on the responsibilities of a king. The Chorus preceding Act IV describes how Henry wanders through the camp

> With [such] cheerful semblance and sweet
>     majesty;
> That every wretch, pining and pale before,
> Beholding him, plucks comfort from his looks.
> A largess universal, like the sun,
> His liberal eye doth give to every one,
> Thawing cold fear, that mean and gentle all
> Behold, as may unworthiness define,
> A little touch of Harry in the night.

Henry, incognito, has a conversation with two soldiers, Bates and Williams, in which the king states that men should be contented to die in the king's company, "his cause being just and his quarrel honorable." Williams counters with the remark that "if the cause be not good, the king himself hath a heavy reckoning to make when all those legs and arms and heads, chopped off in a battle, shall join together" on judgment day and cry out in remonstrance. Henry, alone again, feels overwhelmed by the responsibility that his men place upon him and by the heart's ease that kings must give up in their ceremonial public role.

As a wise and clement leader, Henry has given orders that French rights and property be respected. For, as he observes, "when lenity and cruelty play for a kingdom, the gentler gamester is the soonest winner." Therefore he confirms the death sentence for Bardolph (one of his former associates in Eastcheap), who is guilty of robbing a church. However, when the French, as reprisal for their defeat, set upon the defenseless baggage camp and kill all the boys who have it in charge, the king is relentless in anger:

I was not angry since I came to France
Until this instant.

He gives orders to cut the throats of the prisoners
the English have taken and to spare the life of none of
the enemy whom they may yet encounter on the field.

The battle over, the play leaps to the wooing of
Katherine of France that had been promised in the
epilogue to *2 Henry IV*. This scene is a letdown because of the change of tone and because of the apparent boorishness of the suitor. Yet it does enhance
Henry's image and does provide a triumphant ending
to the play. That he has conquered France is made
clear by French acceptance of all his terms and by
Katherine's acceptance of him as husband. There is
ceremony as well as clowning in this final scene. The
clowning must be seen as incidental, for when the
negotiators reappear upon the stage, there is instant
reversion to regality. As conqueror and inheritor of
France, King Henry V is now raised to a towering
height.

With his characteristic mixture of genres, Shakespeare supplements the epic account of King Henry V
by two series of comic episodes that are only casually
related to the main action. The first group of ancillary
characters consists of four officers in the English
army, Captains Gower and Fluellen, who are Welsh;
Captain Macmorris, who is Irish; and Captain Jamy, a
Scot. They are all stubborn, disputatious, ardent prac-
titioners of the art of war. These men are given to
bickering and earnest, if somewhat irrelevant, phi-
losophizing. Unfortunately, their dialects make them
almost unintelligible. It is idle to argue that in some
way this comic distraction celebrates the racial elements of which Britain is made up, since none of the
ethnic representatives comes off particularly well. It is

wiser to see these characters merely as racial stereotypes, which are generally good for a laugh by reason
of language and behavior patterns that deviate from
the norm accepted by the audience.

The other comic action brings King Henry's former lowlife cronies on stage, but without Falstaff (in
spite of the promise made at the end of *2 Henry IV*).
These scenes lack the ebullience that Falstaff brought
to the earlier plays. The Eastcheap characters are sordid and unredeemed by wit or genial humanity. The
one exception is the great comic interlude in which
Mistress Quickly reports the death of Falstaff to Pistol, Nym, and Bardolph in a wonderful mixture of
sentiment, bawdry, and malapropism. However much
of a birdbrain she may be, she has a good heart and
can feel for others. But braggart Pistol and scrofulous
Nym and Bardolph provide only bitter comedy. They
stand for base animal man, whose only interest in war
is plunder and enjoyment. We see them for what they
are when Pistol in his farewell to London exhorts
them:

> Yoke-fellows in arms,
> Let us to France, like horse-leeches, my boys,
> To suck, to suck, the very blood to suck!
> (II, iii, 49–51)

Thereafter, their course is rapidly downward. Before Harfleur their stance is one of self-interest, under-
lined by the Boy's comment that "three such antics do
not amount to a man," and his determination to leave
them for some better service since they are trying to
corrupt him. Bardolph, as we have seen, is condemned
to death for sacrilege. Pistol plays a cat-and-mouse
game with a French officer whom he has captured at
Agincourt, but fails in his effort to extort money.

Finally, Pistol, having aroused the anger of Fluellen, is forced by the latter to eat a leek, in proof that his braggadocio masks a coward's heart.

This whole sequence is a timely reminder that there is a seamy side to war and that not all warriors are models of knightly valor. It is one of the disquieting elements that make interpretation of the play a problem and lead some twentieth-century readers and producers to go overboard by seeing *Henry V* as an antiwar play, even though the overall structure and emphasis forbid such a reading.

One of the problems in interpreting the play today is that the assumptions on which King Henry's greatness is based are no longer universally accepted. The play is about a war of foreign conquest; thus the achievement is morally suspect, and any reputation that Henry achieves may be suspect as well. His dauntless exhortations as military cheerleader leave us cold. We have had too much experience of filling the wall up with the conscripted dead. Beyond this, the play contains an implicit irony that reflects on the conquest of France. Henry receives assurance from the Archbishop of Canterbury that the so-called Salic Law—forbidding succession to the crown through the female line—has no force in France. Therefore, it is all right for Henry to go ahead and endeavor by force of arms to assert his claim, which comes through the female line. Yet in Act II he quickly and brutally puts down the conspiracy of Richard Earl of Cambridge, who claims that the English crown should have descended through the female line from Edward III's third son Lionel, whereas Henry's claim is through the fourth son. Henry cannot have it both ways logically, but the play quietly skips over this by obscuring Richard's motives.

One of the passages that suggest a satiric approach is the echo of Henry's "Once more into the breach" speech, first by Bardolph and then by Fluellen. The effect of this repetition is not deflationary, however. In the first instance, it allows Nym in reply to indicate his lack of valor and the whole group to drag their feet while their betters are valiantly going forward. In Fluellen's case, it serves to introduce him as a doughty warrior and to give an emphatic example of his peculiar pronunciation: "Up to the preach, you dogs!" If this echo device were part of the entire framework of the play, the case for devaluation of patriotic sentiments would be strong. One instance, however tantalizing, is not enough.

There is one episode that it is impossible to reconcile with the generally heroic tone of the play. This is a conversation between Fluellen and Gower (IV, vii) immediately after the killing of the boys tending the baggage and Henry's angry order to kill all prisoners in reprisal. Gower exclaims enthusiastically: "O, 'tis a gallant king!" By an incredible associative leap, Fluellen replies:

> Ay, he was porn at Monmouth, Captain Gower. What call you the town's name where Alexander the Pig was born?
>
> (IV, vii, 11–13)

Fluellen then proceeds with a parallel between King Henry and Alexander the Great based on trivial facts, but concluding: "If you mark Alexander's life well, Harry of Monmouth's life is come after it [parallels it] indifferent [fairly] well; for there is figures [patterns] in all things." Fluellen then mentions Alexander's killing of his best friend Cleitus, setting the stage for Gower's protest that King Harry never killed any of his friends. Fluellen moves in for the kill, extending the parallel in an unexpected way:

As Alexander killed his friend Cleitus, being in his ales and his cups, so also Harry Monmouth, being in his right wits and his good judgments, turned away the fat knight with the great pelly doublet. He was full of jests and gipes, and knaveries, and mocks. I have forgot his name.

(IV, vii, 40–45)

When reminded that the name is Falstaff, Fluellen concludes: "I'll tell you there is good men porn at Monmouth." King Harry then enters and repeats his vengeful promise to cut the throats of all the prisoners.

The epithet Alexander the Pig is too emphatic for us to overlook it, and the comparison between the killing of Cleitus and the rejection of Falstaff too dragged in for us to ascribe it to whimsy. Here at the high point of King Harry's military achievement we are struck in the face by an incongruous observation that casts doubt upon that achievement—an observation for which there has been no adequate buildup and from which nothing follows. There is no more puzzling passage in all of Shakespeare.

Many readers and spectators, even if they accept Henry as a great leader and a great king, are chilled by the limitations that this greatness seems to entail. They complain that in spite of Shakespeare's efforts to soften the portrait, Henry lacks humanity, in his rejection of Falstaff and the others whom he has misled as to his true nature, in his toying with the Southampton conspirators, and in his oafish wooing of Katherine. Such critics see him as a cold fish, a fire-eater, and possibly a hypocrite in his moral sentiments. Part of this response is due to lack of subtlety in characterization. Henry is too direct, too efficient, too uncomplicated to be attractive.

Perhaps this lukewarm response is also due to the

nature of the language in this play. The Chorus, who appears as prologue to each act, uses a declamatory style more suitable to epic poetry than to drama and therefore sets a hyperbolic tone for the whole work. This declamatory style is not unpleasing. It adds an interesting verbal dimension to a play that does not have much dramatic tension, though at the same time it slows the pace and makes the performance too static and monumental.

What is less easy to accept is the long-windedness of the speeches. The two speeches by the Archbishop of Canterbury in the second scene are notorious for their length and prosy rambling. The Olivier film, not to mention other productions, tries to make this prolixity bearable by introducing stage business among the by-standers that turns the prelate into a figure of fun. This is unfortunate in that the speeches are a serious effort to provide moral justification for the invasion of France. Only if the entire play were satiric could this scene be played as comedy.

Much more important is the tendency of King Henry to deliver himself in lengthy orations, one of thirty-nine lines in answer to the French ambassador, one of sixty-six lines to the conspirators. There is a very long prose rejoinder to the soldier Williams about kingship, followed by a fifty-five-line soliloquy on the same subject. Even the wooing of Katherine is clogged by two very long prose speeches. It does not matter that these speeches are often moving and elo-quent and are received with applause. They are set pieces, not part of the dramatic give and take. They constitute a considerable decline from the quick thrust and parry of the dialogue in the best of the history plays.

The fact remains that *Henry V* has always been one of the most popular of Shakespeare's plays. It was one of the first to be revived when the theaters were re-opened in 1660. There were twenty-four productions of it at Stratford-on-Avon before 1950. Because of its popularity, it was the play chosen by the Royal Shakespeare Theatre for performance in the United States during the bicentennial celebration. And under Laurence Olivier's direction it has yielded us what, by common consent, is the best cinematic version of a Shakespearean play.

## The First Part of
## King Henry the Sixth

When Henry V died in the fall of 1422, his son, Henry VI, now king of both England and France, was less than a year old. His reign (1422–1460; 1470–1471) was long, chaotic, and disastrous for the royal family and for England.

Shakespeare's three plays that attempt to cover the events of Henry VI's reign are simply three segments of a continuous dramatized chronicle, cut into more or less equal lengths for the convenience of production. Dramatic intensity is submerged by historical fact as the plays introduce an overwhelming number of characters and encompass too many historical actions. These works, the first of Shakespeare's efforts in this genre, are his weakest, but they do have interest because of the power of individual episodes and because of the overall picture of political disorder—eventually a civil war—that they present.

Part One covers roughly twenty years of Henry VI's reign, from the death of his father to the young king's engagement to Margaret of Anjou in 1444. The predominant subject of the play is the loss of France, with a secondary focus on the growth of political faction at home.

By the terms of the Treaty of Troyes (1420) the infant Henry VI was also king of France, since his grandfather, Charles VI of France, had died earlier in 1422. Charles's son, referred to as the Dauphin in the play, had been disinherited by the treaty, but the French nobility immediately rallied to his support and in effect repudiated their feudal oaths to the English king. What might be called a national war of liberation was carried on against the English for thirty years. The first great French successes were achieved under the inspiration and leadership of Joan of Arc, who had the Dauphin officially crowned as Charles VII at Reims in 1429.

Even though Joan of Arc was captured in 1430 and, after a trial for heresy, burned by the English at Rouen on May 30, 1431, French successes continued. Paris was recaptured in 1436, Rouen in 1449, and the last major holdings around Bordeaux fell when the English general, Talbot, was killed in battle on July 17, 1453. Except for the fortress city of Calais, the English had lost all the territories in France that had come to them from William the Conqueror (as Duke of Normandy), Geoffrey of Anjou (the father of Henry II), and Elinor of Aquitaine (wife of Henry II), not to mention the more recent conquests of Edward III and Henry V. Almost four centuries of English rule and imperial expansion across the Channel had come to an end.

In an effort to give some degree of dramatic unity to the play, Shakespeare mixes up chronology and telescopes events in a highhanded way. He makes the death of Talbot (1453) precede that of Joan of Arc (1431). The sieges and captures of various cities are not necessarily historical. But the overall picture is accurate enough: What Henry V had inherited or acquired was, within a generation, lost by the incompetence and factionalism of his successors.

Since Henry VI was a minor for most of the period covered in Part One, the fault was obviously not his, but that of his elders. Three major factions of the royal family were continually at odds with one another, trying to fill the power vacuum existing during the young king's minority. Before his death Henry V designated his brother, John Duke of Bedford, as regent of France, and his other brother, Humphrey Duke of Gloucester, as protector of England. They worked well enough together for more than a decade until John died in 1435, though the kingdom was already being troubled by additional ambitious uncles— to be precise, great-half-uncles.

John of Gaunt (Duke of Lancaster and founder of the Lancastrian line), by a liaison with Katherine Swynford, a lady of his mother's court, had sired three illegitimate sons, who were given the name Beaufort. After they reached maturity, John of Gaunt was able to marry their mother. The Pope pronounced them legitimate in 1395, as did Richard II, whose act was confirmed by Parliament in 1397. However, the Beauforts were declared outside the line of succession to the crown. The oldest, John, became Duke of Somerset; the second, Henry, became Bishop of Winchester and was later made a cardinal; the third, Thomas, was Duke of Exeter. (A sister, Joan, married Ralph Neville, first Earl of Westmoreland, by whom she had nine surviving children. The youngest of these, Cicely, married Richard Duke of York and became the mother of Edward IV and Richard III, outliving both of them.)

The Beaufort brothers were ambitious. In spite of their original illegitimacy they considered themselves of royal blood. Since Henry IV had no other brothers, they demanded and obtained high place during his reign and that of Henry V. On his deathbed the latter indicated that Henry Beaufort and Thomas Beaufort were to have charge of Henry VI's upbringing and education. This charge gave them a privileged position and brought them into collision with Humphrey Duke of Gloucester, the protector. With the passage of time the Beaufort heirs, forgetting their illegitimate origin, thought of themselves as true Lancastrians with a legitimate claim on the crown.

There was still a third faction of utmost importance. Henry IV, who usurped the throne in 1399, claimed it through his father, John of Gaunt, the *fourth* son of Edward III. However, the *third* son, Lionel Duke of Clarence, was survived by a daughter who, in default of a law to the contrary, could claim the crown by primogeniture. Indeed, her grandson, Edmund Mortimer, was designated by Richard II as his heir. During the reign of Henry IV, the Percy rebellion was at least ostensibly on behalf of Mortimer, as was the conspiracy mounted by Richard Earl of Cambridge under Henry V.

With the death of the last male Mortimer in 1425, events took a new turn. The descendants of the Duke of York, Edward III's *fifth* son, became active claimants, not primarily in virtue of their descent from York but by reason of descent through the female line from Lionel Duke of Clarence.

Indeed it was this claim that Richard Earl of Cambridge was asserting in 1415 on behalf of his wife, the sister of Edmund Mortimer. The Earl of Cambridge was beheaded, and his descendants were put under attainder, that is, deprived of titles and property. However, under Henry VI rights were restored to Cambridge's son Richard, who was created Duke of York. He laid the groundwork for assuming the crown during the period covered by *1 Henry VI*, was killed before he achieved his goal during the civil war that attended his efforts. But he did win the kingdom for his sons Edward IV and Richard III. The lineup in the

Lancastrian-Yorkist conflict thus becomes clear. Henry VI was a Lancastrian, as his father, grandfather, and great-grandfather had been. He had as allies, at least part of the time, the members of the Beaufort clan, who were also Lancastrians. The Yorkists were represented by Richard Duke of York by reason of his descent through the female line from Edward III's third son, a claim buttressed, of course, by the fact that he was also the grandson of Edmund Duke of York, Edward III's fifth son. The contestants were all cousins. The so-called Wars of the Roses were a family affair, but no less bitter and brutal on that account.

The first scene of *1 Henry VI* provides the basis for both the major actions of the play. Around Henry V's coffin stand his two brothers, John Duke of Bedford and Humphrey Duke of Gloucester, and his three Beaufort relatives. In the midst of their grief Gloucester cannot refrain from needling the Bishop of Winchester (one of his Beaufort uncles), who returns the insults with interest. This conflict is arrested by the arrival of three successive messengers, each bringing news of grievous setbacks in France. (These anticipate actual historical events by several years, but their impact is dramatic as well as premonitory.) One messenger points out that factionalism at home is partly responsible for the disasters abroad and exhorts the English leaders:

> Awake, awake, English nobility!
> Let not sloth dim your honors new begot.
> Cropped are the flower-de-luces in your arms;
> Of England's coat one half is cut away.
> (I, i, 78–81)

Two later scenes develop the animosity between the Bishop of Winchester and Humphrey Duke of Gloucester. In I, iii, their retainers brawl in the streets until the Lord Mayor of London is forced to quell the disturbance and to rebuke the two leaders. This brawling is repeated in III, i. This time King Henry VI (who is actually only about five years old) precociously attempts to reconcile his uncles and points out that

> Civil dissension is a viperous worm
> That gnaws the bowels of the commonwealth.
> (III, i, 72–73)

Meanwhile, in a famous symbolic scene, sides are taken among the courtiers for the eventual dynastic war. In II, iv, we see a group of young men arguing in the garden of the Temple (one of the law schools in London). Richard Plantagenet, the Yorkist heir, and the Duke of Somerset, a Beaufort and Lancastrian, dispute the legitimacy of the Yorkist claim. Those who believe in the Yorkist claim pluck a white rose; Somerset and Suffolk, who deny it, pluck a red rose. Even though Richard of York has, so to speak, a majority vote, Somerset refuses to abide by it. When asked, "Where is your argument?" he answers:

> Here in my scabbard, meditating that
> Shall dye your white rose in a bloody red.
> (II, iv, 60–61)

These young men will become the protagonists of the bloody wars to follow: Somerset and Suffolk on the side of the Lancastrians; York and the redoubtable Earl of Warwick on the Yorkist side.

The validity of York's claim is reemphasized in the following scene, where he visits his dying uncle, Edmund Mortimer, in prison. (Holinshed and Shakespeare are in error. Edmund Mortimer was not imprisoned but loyally served the crown in Ireland until his death.) Having rehearsed the genealogical data supporting Richard's claim, the uncle dies. Richard determines to act more forcefully in defense of his rights than the unenergetic Mortimer and to demand a restoration of his lands and titles from Parliament. In a scene at court, Henry VI creates him Duke of York, while Somerset mutters angrily in the background. Still later (IV, i), there is a confrontation between York and Somerset in the king's presence. Henry VI undertakes to be umpire in their strife, unwisely asserting:

> I see no reason, if I wear this rose,
> That any one should therefore be suspicious
> I more incline to Somerset than York.
> (IV, i, 152–54)

His statement is naive, since it is the red rose he has chosen. And his decision to make York regent of France, with Somerset in a position under him, does nothing to alleviate the tension. In fact, the impossibility of cooperation between the two adversaries is shown to be the principal cause of the defeat and death of Talbot, the English general at Bordeaux.

In presenting the scenes of battle in France—the major action of the play—Shakespeare makes Lord Talbot the protagonist and Joan of Arc his chief antagonist. This is grossly unhistorical. Except for a six-week period in the spring of 1429, they were not aligned against each other, since Talbot was captured at the battle of Patay in May 1429 and not released until 1433, when Joan had been dead for two years. It is dramatically fitting, however, that the two heroic figures be pitted against each other.

Talbot receives a tremendous build-up. In the account of his capture, the messenger tells of the three-hour fight

> Where valiant Talbot above human thought
> Enacted wonders with his sword and lance.
> Hundreds he sent to hell, and none durst stand
>     him;
> Here, there, and everywhere enraged he slew.
> The French exclaimed the devil was in arms;
> All the whole army stood agazed on him.
>
> (I, i, 121–26)

Bested by Joan in their first encounter at Orléans, Talbot turns the tables, scaling the walls of the city as the French lie sleeping. The French provide a ludicrous sight as they escape, leaping from the walls in their nightshirts. One English soldier comments that he has used the name of Talbot as a sword,

> For I have loaden me with many spoils,
> Using no other weapon but his name.

The French scatter like sheep before the name, let alone the person, of the English hero.

Two scenes give a view of Talbot in less warlike circumstances. The Countess of Auvergne invites him into a trap, intending to capture him in her own house, only to find that he has not come unattended. Moreover, she twits him for his unattractive physique:

> I thought I should have seen some Hercules,
> A second Hector, for his grim aspect
> And large proportion of his strong-knit limbs.
> Alas, this is a child, a silly dwarf.
> It cannot be this weak and writhled shrimp
> Should strike such terror to his enemies.
>
> (II, iii, 19–24)

Then she readily capitulates to his charms.

In III, iv, Talbot meets Henry VI for the first time. The warrior shows himself loyal and submissive to his sovereign—in marked contrast with the other haughty lords who surround the king. Henry speaks with awe of this legendary soldier, of whom he says he had heard his father speak with approbation. The king creates Talbot Earl of Shrewsbury and invites him to take his place in the coronation ceremony about to be performed in Paris. Finally, in this scene, Talbot upbraids Sir John Falstaff (not the fat knight of *Henry IV*) for his notorious cowardice and tears the insignia of the Order of the Garter from his leg.

The decline of English fortunes in France is marked by three poignant death scenes. In I, iv, the Earl of Salisbury, a hero of Henry V's campaigns, is killed by a random shot before Orléans. His death is accompanied by tumult in the heavens, as Talbot vows revenge:

> Frenchmen, I'll be a Salisbury to you.
> Pucelle or pussel, Dolphin or dogfish,
> Your hearts I'll stamp out with my horse's
>     heels
> And make a quagmire of your mingled brains.
>                          (I, iv, 106–09)

At the siege of Rouen (III, ii) the successful English assault is marred by the death of John of Bedford, the regent of France. This causes Talbot to make the melancholy observation that

> . . . kings and mightiest potentates must die,
> For that's the end of human misery.
>                          (III, ii, 136–37)

These two scenes are preparation for the grand finale of Talbot's death (IV, v, vi, vii). Here Shakespeare pulls out all the stops in a long farewell to English supremacy in France. The English armies are encircled by the French with no hope of escape because of Somerset's failure to come to their aid in time. Once more it is English faction, not French force of arms, that brings the English down. Talbot, facing the inevitable, urges his son, John Talbot, to escape. The son refuses. Talbot, mortally wounded, receives the dead body of his son in his arms and dies. The French want to hack Talbot's body to pieces, but Charles VII, for once exercising judgment and forbearance, forbids this:

> O, no, forbear! For that which we have fled
> During the life, let us not wrong it dead.
> (IV, vii, 49–50)

Sir William Lucy, an English leader, cites Talbot's titles and achievements in passionate requiem. The scene concludes with Charles's jubilant promise:

> All will be ours, now bloody Talbot's slain.
> (IV, vii, 96)

Shakespeare's treatment of Joan of Arc has offended latter-day sensibilities. His view, of course, is simply partisan. Joan is not saint and virgin but a sorceress, a limb of Satan, since only evil supernatural force would be able to bring the English down. In fact, Shakespeare pretty much follows Holinshed in his assessment and portrayal:

> Of favor was she counted likesome, of person strongly made and manly, of courage great, hardy,

and stout withal: an understander of counsels though she were not at them; great semblance of chastity both of body and behavior; the name of Jesus in her mouth about all her business; humble, obedient; and fasting divers days in the week. A person (as their books make her) raised up by power divine, only for succor to the French estate then deeply in distress. . . .

The play presents the famous scene of legend, where Joan spied out the Dauphin hiding, as a test, among a group of courtiers. It shows her in frequent collision with Talbot, boasting, jeering, and warning him that she will be his nemesis. Talbot in turn calls her strumpet and witch. There is a continuing strain of sexual innuendo in her scenes with Charles VII. Nonetheless, in the first part of the play she is undeniably a heroic figure and a rallying force of great assistance to the French cause.

It is in the final scenes of Joan's life that Shakespeare goes all out in defamation. She summons up demonic figures to aid her and to foretell the future. After her capture she denies her peasant father, declaring that she is "descended of a gentler blood." He in turn berates her, urging the English to burn her, since "hanging is too good." To delay execution, she asserts that she is pregnant. To the jeers of her captors, she names the Dauphin, then Alençon, then Réné, King of Naples, as the father of her child. She goes to her execution with a curse upon the English:

> May never glorious sun reflex his beams
> Upon the country where you make abode;
> But darkness and the gloomy shade of death
> Environ you, till mischief and despair
> Drive you to break your necks or hang
> yourselves!
>
> (V, iv, 87–91)

Even for this intemperate and ribald treatment, there is basis in Holinshed, who reports that the ecclesiastical authorities before whom Joan was taken after her capture condemned her for "shamefully rejecting her sex abominably in acts and apparel" and for being "a pernicious instrument to hostility and bloodshed in devilish witchcraft and sorcery." Having promised to "cast off her unnatural wearing of man's habiliments, and keep her to garments of her own kind, abjure her pernicious practices of sorcery and witchcraft," she fell "straightway into her former abominations, (and yet seeking to eke out life as long as she might,) stake not [was not ashamed] . . . to confess herself a strumpet, and (unmarried as she was) to be with child." Holinshed righteously concluded that the Dauphin's "dignity abroad [was] foully spotted in this point, that, contrary to the holy degree of a right Christian prince (as he called himself), for maintenance of his quarrels in war [he] would not reverence to profane his sacred estate, as dealing in devilish practices with misbelievers and witches."

Logically, the deaths of Talbot and Joan of Arc should end the play. However, there is one further action—the wooing of Margaret of Anjou by the Earl of Suffolk in behalf of Henry VI, who has reached an age where he takes a conscientious, if not hot-blooded, interest in girls. While these scenes primarily look forward to the succeeding plays, in which Margaret as queen will be a leading figure on the Lancastrian side, they also remind us of the two major emphases of this play. Not only does Margaret come without a dowry, but Henry VI actually gives over some of his French provinces to her father—one more diminution of the English empire in France. And Suffolk, riding high in royal favor and suspecting from Margaret's demurely flirtatious behavior that he may gain her favors also, enters the lists as a principal in the contest to see who will actually rule the kingdom. As the play ends, he complacently observes:

> Thus Suffolk hath prevailed; and thus he goes,
> As did the youthful Paris once to Greece,
> With hope to find the like event in love
> But prosper better than the Trojan did.
> Margaret shall now be queen, and rule the
>     king;
> But I will rule both her, the king, and realm.
>
> (V, v, 103–08)

## The Second Part of
## King Henry the Sixth

This play is more tightly organized and more dramatic than its predecessor. Long on rhetoric and stage effects, but short on nuancing of character, it is a melodrama of political intrigue ending in open civil war.

The period covered is a ten-year span from the arrival of Queen Margaret in England in the spring of 1445 (she had been married by proxy to Henry VI at Tours the previous November) to the Battle of St. Albans on May 22, 1455. Four major events are dramatized: the disgrace of Eleanor Duchess of Gloucester (which actually occurred earlier, in 1441); the dismissal and murder of Humphrey Duke of Gloucester, the Lord Protector, in 1447; Jack Cade's rebellion, a proletarian uprising, in 1450; and the outbreak of military conflict between the Lancastrian and Yorkist factions at St. Albans in 1455, when for the first time Henry VI's rule was overtly challenged.

Queen Margaret is the new factor, the catalyst, that brings factionalism to a boil. But it is also significant that the passage of time has demonstrated that Henry VI will never be a strong king. This recognition spurs the various ambitious nobles to seek to control him and to exercise power through him. Inevitably their ambitions collide. There are transitory alliances among unlikely partners. Overall, however, the line of division is clearly drawn. On the one hand are the Lancastrians headed by the energetic queen, with Cardinal Beaufort and the Dukes of Somerset, Suffolk, and Buckingham exerting strong influence. On the other is Richard Duke of York in alliance with the powerful Neville family, represented by the Earl of Salisbury and his son the Earl of Warwick (York's wife is also a Neville). At the end of the play, with considerable historical license, Shakespeare also brings York's two sons, Edward and Richard, into the fray.

Three new seekers after power have a predominant place in this play. The paramount position of Suffolk (created duke in 1448) was prefigured at the end of *1 Henry VI*. Now we see him in full sway, dominating the queen and through her the king, asserting at one point that there is no need to consult King Henry since he and others are in agreement. Suffolk is the only one of the chief contestants for power who is not a member of the royal family, but he comports himself with as much arrogance as a real Plantagenet.

Another newcomer to the power stakes is Humphrey Stafford, created first Duke of Buckingham in 1444. He is the grandson of Thomas Duke of Gloucester, the sixth of Edward III's sons, whom Richard II caused to be murdered in 1397. Though his descent is through the female line and his branch is the lowest on the royal family tree, he and his descendants have their own dreams of glory about acceding to the throne. In the meantime, he is willing to ally himself with whoever can diminish the power of the protector, Humphrey Duke of Gloucester.

Finally, there is the Earl of Warwick, Richard of

York's nephew, whose astuteness and military capacity earn him the nickname of the Kingmaker. After Warwick and his father, the Earl of Salisbury, come over to York's side, the stage is set for action. York has the most powerful family in England behind him, and he has assurance of prompt military support if he decides to force a showdown with the Lancastrians.

In contrast with the unscrupulous maneuvering for power of the queen and the various nobles is the selfless concern for the kingdom of Humphrey Duke of Gloucester. He has held England together during the long minority of Henry VI. He has put a rein on the ambitions of Cardinal Beaufort, the Duke of Somerset, and the Duke of York. When Queen Margaret, Suffolk, and Buckingham enter the power game, they are quick to recognize that Duke Humphrey is an obstacle whom they must remove. Humphrey is good; they are therefore evil. Humphrey is constant in his concern for England; their concern is only for themselves. Humphrey stands for order and continuity. By their ambition they undermine order and fracture continuity. Humphrey is a reproach to their heedless egotism; therefore all the aspirants for power are in agreement on one point: Humphrey has to go.

The opening scene initiates their intrigues. Humphrey, appalled at the terms of the marriage with Margaret, leaves the room lest his anger get out of hand. Cardinal Beaufort suggests that Humphrey really wants to usurp the kingdom. Buckingham eagerly suggests that it is time to end the protectorship, and the cardinal dashes off to talk to Suffolk about this. Somerset observes that there is danger that the cardinal will replace the protector in a position of supreme power, but Buckingham sees no reason why he himself or Somerset might not become supreme.

Left alone, the Earl of Salisbury, his son Warwick, and the Duke of York piously comment that

> While these do labor for their own preferment,
> Behooves it us to labor for the realm.
>
> (I, i, 179–80)

Salisbury, who appears to be disinterested, urges

> Join we together for the public good,
> In what we can to bridle and suppress
> The pride of Suffolk and the cardinal
> With Somerset's and Buckingham's ambition;
> And, as we may, cherish Duke Humphrey's
> deeds
> While they do tend the profit of the land.
>
> (I, i, 197–202)

York subscribes to these sentiments, but in a long soliloquy he makes his real purposes clear:

> A day will come when York shall claim his
> own;
> And therefore I will take the Nevils' parts,
> And make a show of love to proud Duke
> Humphrey,
> And when I spy advantage, claim the crown,
> For that's the golden mark I seek to hit.
>
> (I, i, 237–41)

Duke Humphrey's qualities as ruler are shown in two incidental scenes involving the common people. In the first, an apprentice charges his master with having uttered treasonable remarks favorable to the Duke of York. Without judging the case, Humphrey concludes that it would be unwise to send York back to France as regent until the matter is cleared up. In another scene, the royal party encounters a scamp named Simpcox, who claims that his sight has been miraculously restored. The pious King Henry is ready to believe the miracle and to line Simpcox's pockets. Humphrey is not taken in. By close questioning he casts doubts on the man's blindness and, for good measure, proves he is not a cripple, for at the threat of a whipping Simpcox runs away in nimble fashion.

The first move to bring about Humphrey's downfall is directed against his wife, who is shown to be arrogant and covetous of the honor of being queen. Suffolk and Buckingham set a trap for her, in which she is caught summoning up spirits in order to hear what the future has in store. She is disgraced and banished for impiety and treason. With his usual rectitude, her husband does not use his power in her behalf. Humphrey bids his wife farewell as she penitentially walks barefoot through the streets of London. She upbraids him for not saving her from shame and warns that

> . . . Suffolk—he that can do all in all
> With her that hateth thee and hates us all—
> And York and impious Beaufort, that false
>     priest,
> Have all limed bushes to betray thy wings,
> And fly thou how thou canst, they'll tangle
>     thee.
>
> (II, iv, 51–55)

In fact, in the preceding scene King Henry has already demanded that Humphrey give up his staff of office as protector. The queen continues to poison the king's mind about Humphrey's desire to usurp the crown. Suffolk, Cardinal Beaufort, York, and Buckingham all chime in with charges of their own. Suffolk soon arrests Humphrey and places him in the custody of the cardinal while awaiting trial. Addressing the king, Humphrey attempts to warn of what is to come:

I know their complot is to have my life,
And if my death might make this island happy
And prove the period of their tyranny,
I would expend it with all willingness.
But mine is made the prologue to their play,
For thousands more, that yet suspect no peril,
Will not conclude their plotted tragedy.

(III, i, 147–53)

King Henry, shattered by what has befallen and un-
convinced that Humphrey is guilty of treason, quits
the room, leaving the queen and her adherents to plot
further mischief. It is Queen Margaret who does not
hesitate to give words to what they are all thinking:

This Gloucester should be quickly rid the
world,
To rid us from the fear we have of him.

(III, i, 233–34)

Suffolk speaks energetically in favor of killing Humphrey without trial; the cardinal undertakes to find the
executioner. They all shake hands in self-congratula-
tory agreement.

The repercussions of the murder are immediate.
Even such an innocent as Henry VI suspects foul play.
Salisbury and Warwick, backed by members of the
House of Commons, demand to see the body, which is
drawn forth on stage. Popular resentment is so fierce
that the king is forced to exile Suffolk. (Historically
this punishment did not take place until three years
after Humphrey's death.) When the queen pleads for
her lover, the king gives her an unexpectedly strong
rebuke and stands firm. The tearful farewell of Margaret and Suffolk is interrupted by word that Cardinal
Beaufort has been stricken with madness and is on the

point of death. Nemesis is overtaking both the chief perpetrators of Humphrey's murder.

Suffolk is captured on board the ship by which he is leaving England. His haughty pleas for life do not impress his captors, who cut off his head on the shore. Two scenes later (IV, iv), Queen Margaret comes on stage with Suffolk's by now well-preserved head cradled in her arms. For once her mind is not on intrigue as she laments:

> Here may his head lie on my throbbing breast,
> But where's the body that I should embrace?
>
> (IV, iv, 5–6)

The liveliest part of this play is a sequence of nine scenes (IV, ii to x) that present or refer to the Cade Rebellion. Early on, the Duke of York has announced in soliloquy:

> I have seduced a headlong Kentishman,
> John Cade of Ashford,
> To make commotion, as full well he can,
> Under the title of John Mortimer . . .
> By this I shall perceive the commons' mind,
> How they affect the house and claim of York.
> Say he be taken, racked, and tortured;
> I know no pain they can inflict upon him
> Will make him say I moved him to those arms.
> Say that he thrive, as 'tis great like he will;
> Why, then from Ireland come I with my
>   strength
> And reap the harvest which that rascal sowed;
> For, Humphrey being dead, as he shall be,
> And Henry put apart, the next for me.
>
> (III, i, 356–59; 374–83)

Cade and his followers disport themselves with a combination of native wit and appalling random violence. They are likeable rascals for their ability to translate the abstractions of power into the realities of food, drink, and personal privilege. But they are also levelers. They capture a village clerk and, because he can read and write, put him to death. They have it in for Lord Say, whom they accuse of having sold out in France: "and more than that, he can speak French, and therefore he is a traitor." They strike off the heads of Lord Say and his son-in-law, Sir James Cromer, and parade through the streets of London, making the severed heads kiss at each corner. Cade orders his followers to pull down the Savoy, to level the Inns of Court, and to destroy all the records of the realm, for, he says, "My mouth shall be the parliament of England."

As always in Shakespeare, the rabble are to be despised for their inconstancy. They are easily won away from Cade by slogans and by the king's offer of amnesty. Cade goes into hiding, and after several days is discovered and killed by Alexander Iden, a Kentish gentleman. Iden utters appropriate sentiments of horror at Cade's subversion of decent order:

> Die, damned wretch, the curse of her that bare
> thee!
> And as I thrust thy body in with my sword,
> So wish I, I might thrust thy soul to hell!
> Hence will I drag thee headlong by the heels
> Unto a dunghill, which shall be thy grave,
> And there cut off thy most ungracious head,
> Which I will bear in triumph to the king,
> Leaving thy trunk for crows to feed upon.
>
> (IV, x, 75–82)

The king, much edified by this exhibition of God's providence, gazes piously on Cade's head and knights Iden in reward for his valor.

The realistic speech and actions of Jack Cade and his fellows are in pleasant contrast with the often windy posturings of the nobles. These scenes are recognizably human and often funny. They remind us that the animosities of late feudal England were felt by real people, that there was passion, more than histrionic attitudes, beneath the chain mail and the velvet of kings and nobles. However, these scenes have a more important function than that of humanizing the action. They show disorder at large in the land on a lower level, concomitant with and the direct outcome of disorder on the highest level. When there is a weak king, when the nobles are at odds with the king and with one another, such chaos is the result. And in Alexander Iden, who brings Cade's derelictions to an end, we have an exemplar of a sense of duty and contentment, from whom the warring nobles might learn a lesson. In a soliloquy, Iden provides a vignette of humble well-being, of a little Eden, to emphasize the pun in his name:

> Lord, who would live turmoiled in the court
> And may enjoy such quiet walks as these?
> This small inheritance my father left me
> Contenteth me, and worth a monarchy.
> I seek not to wax great by others' waning,
> Or gather wealth, I care not with what envy.
> Sufficeth that I have maintains my state
> And send the poor well pleased from my gate.
> (IV, x, 15–22)

With Cardinal Beaufort and the Duke of Suffolk out of the way, the Duke of York has only one formidable obstacle in his path among the nobility. Telescoping several years' maneuvering, Shakespeare presents the Duke of York forcing the removal of the

Duke of Somerset from power. The king breaks faith at the queen's insistent urging and allows Somerset to come back to court. York is at last moved to action. Warwick, Salisbury, and York's two sons array themselves against the embattled Lancastrians led by the queen, Somerset, and Lord Clifford. In a battle fought at St. Albans, only a few miles north of London, Richard, York's son, kills Somerset. (Historically, he was only three years old at the time.) York kills Lord Clifford; the Duke of Buckingham is wounded. The Yorkists have won the first battle in the Wars of the Roses.

Two omissions of historical fact need comment. Henry VI and Queen Margaret were childless for almost a decade. Rumor had it that the king was impotent. And when Prince Edward was born on October 13, 1453—a fact unmentioned by Shakespeare—there were those who asserted that the Duke of Somerset was the father. Whatever the case, up to that point the Duke of York was by primogeniture the heir to the throne. This may well have led him to go slow. After Edward's birth there was no such brake on his actions. With a Lancastrian heir assured, he had to fight for his rights, since they would never come to him automatically.

Shakespeare's other omission is even more interesting. There is not the slightest hint of Henry VI's periodic mental ailment, which presumably he inherited from his grandfather, Charles VI of France, who was similarly afflicted. The English king was stricken for the first time in July 1453 and was in a comatose condition for almost a year and a half. Parliament finally made the Duke of York protector at the end of March 1454. Somerset was arrested and put in the Tower; other Lancastrian officials in high places were swept out. With the recovery of Henry VI, the queen acted energetically, releasing Somerset, who replaced York as protector. (The king had a second and less prolonged attack in the fall of 1455; again York was protector for a few months.) The fact that York, not the queen, was named protector indicates that there was strong support for York in Parliament. The country as well as the Plantagenet dynasty was divided.

Perhaps Shakespeare did not feel it was fitting to represent a king as imbecile. Perhaps he was merely being cautious. The Tudor monarchs were also descended from Charles VI by Katherine of Valois's union with Owen Tudor, the grandfather of Henry VII. It was not wise to cast any shadow on Tudor ancestry, though those monarchs never showed any sign of mental incapacity.

## The Third Part of King Henry the Sixth

During the last ten years of his life, Henry VI was king for only a few months. Thus this play might appropriately be called "King Edward IV." However, the focus is on neither king. Rather the play's subject is the increasing ferocity of civil war. Both factions engage in a frenzy of brutality. The ultimate impact on the spectator or reader is to make him reject both York and Lancaster, to anticipate Mercutio's outburst in *Romeo and Juliet* and say, "A plague on both your houses."

By a neat trick of compression of time, Shakespeare makes the opening of *3 Henry VI* seem to follow immediately on the Yorkist victory at St. Albans in 1455, with which the previous play ends. In fact, it was five years later, after the battle of Northampton on July 10, 1460, that the Yorkists marched on London and Richard Duke of York affronted the Lancastrians by seating himself in the chair of state. In October of that year, a compromise was worked out by which York was named heir to the throne and protector, with the proviso that Henry VI be allowed to remain king for the rest of his life.

Queen Margaret would have none of this. She and her son Edward, the Prince of Wales, raised an army in the north and besieged York at his castle of Sandal. He unwisely gave battle against heavy odds and was killed at Wakefield on December 30, 1460. His second son, the Earl of Rutland, was captured and murdered by young Clifford, whose father had been killed at St. Albans five years before. The Earl of Salisbury (the Earl of Warwick's father) and other prisoners were beheaded. Their heads joined York's on the walls of the city of York. Edward, the Duke of York's oldest son, turned the tables against the Lancastrians at the battle of Towton on March 29, 1461. Henry VI fled to Scotland for sanctuary; Queen Margaret and the Prince of Wales eventually took refuge in France.

Edward of York was crowned king as Edward IV on June 28, 1461. He was nineteen years old.

Only two clusters of events of the next eight years receive treatment in the play. In 1465, Henry VI incautiously ventured back to England; he was captured and imprisoned in the Tower, where he remained until the fall of 1470. Edward IV made an impulsive marriage with Elizabeth Woodville (Lady Grey) in May 1464 while Warwick was in France negotiating a marriage with the French king's sister-in-law.

Shakespeare uses this double-dealing by Edward IV as motivation for Warwick's desertion of the Yorkist party, which is the subject of the last part of the play. In fact, that defection did not take place until the years 1469 and 1470, when Warwick's daughter Anne was married to Edward, the Lancastrian Prince of Wales, and Warwick's older daughter was married to the Yorkist Duke of Clarence, Edward IV's brother. Warwick the Kingmaker, himself descended from the royal family by way of a Beaufort grandmother, had decided that one of his grandchildren would be king.

He hedged his bets by marriages to representatives of both houses.

With Warwick and Clarence in the field on the side of Queen Margaret, Edward IV was captured and imprisoned. Henry VI resumed the throne, appointing Warwick and Clarence joint protectors. He had Parliament declare Edward IV a traitor and stripped him of all his titles and property. These he gave to the Yorkist Duke of Clarence, designating him heir presumptive to the throne if the Prince of Wales should die without issue.

Edward IV escaped from prison and raised an army on the Continent, while his brother Richard rallied support at home. Their brother the Duke of Clarence returned to the fold. Within a month of Edward IV's return to England, Henry VI was a captive again. On May 4, 1471, the Yorkists wreaked full revenge on their adversaries. Edward Prince of Wales was stabbed to death in his mother's sight. The current Duke of Somerset was beheaded. Warwick was killed. Queen Margaret was captured. Less than three weeks after the Tewkesbury battle, Richard of York murdered Henry VI in the Tower. The direct male line of both branches of the Lancastrian house had been extinguished. Edward IV became king again.

The important new figures in this play are Richard Duke of York's four sons. Edward, a typical Plantagenet—tall, blue-eyed, with golden hair—speedily became the darling of the people. He was a great warrior and also a great womanizer. Edmund Earl of Rutland was not the tender lad that Holinshed and Shakespeare make him, but a youth of seventeen when he was murdered at Wakefield. George Duke of Clarence was ambitious and malleable, eager to advance his own interests but lacking the intelligence and will to carry through. Finally, Richard Duke of Gloucester, the youngest son, destined to have his character blackened in perpetuity by Sir Thomas More and Shakespeare, was a fine soldier and potentially a good king. However, he has come down to us as resolute, bloody, and unprincipled, a "murderous Machiavel," as he calls himself in soliloquy.

There is little to distinguish the new generation of Dukes of Somerset or the various members of the Neville family who align themselves with the warring houses. However, under the regime of Edward IV certain new figures take on importance. There is Lord Rivers, Queen Elizabeth's brother, the head of the extensive Woodville connection who greedily seek high place under Edward IV. And there are two nobles who endear themselves by their early help. Lord Hastings becomes chamberlain and is also a rival for the king's mistress, Jane Shore. Lord William Stanley belonged to a family with remarkable powers of survival, whose line has continued without interruption to the present day. Witness the Stanley Cup, goal of competition in the field of hockey, established in 1893 by the then Earl of Derby.

Richard Duke of York's rapid reverse of fortune provides an intensely dramatic opening section of the play. After their success at Northampton, the Yorkists occupy London. The Earl of Warwick vows to "plant Plantagenet, root him up who dares" and urges York to claim the crown. York is seated on the throne when Henry VI enters and demands:

> Thou factious Duke of York, descend my
> throne
> And kneel for grace and mercy at my feet.
> (I, i, 74–75)

The king blusters for a time, until York's sons urge their father to "tear the crown from the usurper's head." King Henry, starting to affirm his right to the crown, breaks off in dismay, saying in an aside, "I know not what to say; my title's weak" (I, i, 134). He quickly capitulates when Warwick (then an ally of the Yorks) summons the armed soldiers whom he has placed in the shadows and entails the crown on York and his heirs forever. Queen Margaret rails against her husband for his weakness:

> The soldiers should have tossed me on their
>     pikes
> Before I would have granted to that act . . .
> And seeing thou dost, I here divorce myself
> Both from thy table, Henry, and thy bed
> Until the act of parliament be repealed
> Whereby my son is disinherited.
> (I, i, 244–50)

York's sons Edward and Richard, impatient over the delay, urge their father to seize the crown at once. Edward says crassly that "for a kingdom any oath may be broken." Richard argues that an oath made to King Henry is null and void because the king, a usurper, has no authority, concluding:

> I cannot rest
> Until the white rose that I wear be dyed
> Even in the lukewarm blood of Henry's heart.
> (I, ii, 32–34)

Richard Duke of York, with heavy dramatic irony, declares that he will be king or die. Almost immediately he hears of the approach of Queen Margaret's army, which will bring him death, not the kingship.

The prelude to the battle is the capture of young Rutland by Clifford. All appeals for mercy fail as Clifford stabs Rutland: "Thy father slew my father.

Therefore die." Queen Margaret prolongs the life of the captured Duke of York so that she can mete out humiliating retaliation. She makes him stand on a molehill with a paper crown on his head as she jeers at him:

> What, was it you that would be England's
>     king?
> Was't you that revelled in our parliament
> And made a preachment of your high descent?
> Where are your mess of sons to back you now?
> The wanton Edward, and the lusty George?
> And where's that valiant crookback prodigy,
> Dicky your boy, that with his grumbling voice
> Was wont to cheer his dad in mutinies?
> Or, with the rest, where is your darling
>     Rutland?
> Look, York! I stained this napkin with the
>     blood
> That valiant Clifford with his rapier's point
> Made issue from the bosom of the boy;
> And if thine eyes can water for his death,
> I give thee this to dry thy cheeks withal.
>                                      (I, iv, 70–83)

Even after ordering York's beheading, Queen Margaret delays execution, hoping for tears and pleas from her victim. Instead, York lashes out at her with invective equal to her own:

> She-wolf of France, but worse than wolves of
>     France,
> Whose tongue more poisons than the adder's
>     tooth,
> How ill-beseeming is it in thy sex
> To triumph like an Amazonian trull
> Upon their woes whom fortune captivates.
> But that thy face is vizard-like, unchanging,

Made impudent with use of evil deeds,
I would assay, proud queen, to make thee
    blush.
To tell thee whence thou cam'st, of whom
    derived,
Were shame enough to shame thee, wert thou
    not shameless.

(I, iv, 111–20)

The scene ends with Margaret and Clifford repeatedly stabbing York, and Margaret ordering

Off with his head and set it on York gates,
So York may overlook the town of York.

(I, iv, 179–80)

When in II, ii, Margaret enters York at the head of her army, she rejoices at the sight of York's head and asks King Henry if the sight does not cheer his heart. Henry is appalled at her bloodthirstiness and prays God not to exact vengeance on him. The ensuing battle is unrelenting on both sides. The Lancastrians are defeated; Clifford is killed. Warwick orders that Clifford's head replace that of the Duke of York on the gate of the city, for

Measure for measure must be answered.

(II, vi, 55)

It is in this atmosphere of personal vendetta that Henry VI, for the first time in the three plays that bear his name, achieves significant stature. When it comes to a shouting match, the king is always shouted down. When it comes to battle, he is always relegated to the sidelines as being an obstacle to successful warfare. Now, in the battle just described, he appears on stage alone, sitting on a molehill as he meditates on the uncertain ebb and flow of battle. He conjures up a vision of a simple pastoral life:

> O God! methinks it were a happy life
> To be no better than a homely swain;

living life governed by the seasons and the tasks that they automatically impose, instead of being a king

> When care, mistrust, and treason waits on him.
> (II, v, 21–22, 54)

As Henry sits in meditation a little moral scene is played out before him. At one door there enters a son who has killed his father, at another a father who has killed his son, each bearing the victim's corpse in his arms. These are the visible results of the internecine struggle between the royal families, a struggle that tears apart the natural bonds of parent and child throughout the whole nation. Henry sees himself as the helpless cause of this unnatural condition:

> Woe above woe, grief more than common
>     grief;
> O that my death would stay these ruthful
>     deeds!
> O, pity, pity, gentle heaven, pity!
> The red rose and the white are on his face,
> The fatal colors of our striving houses.
> The one his purple blood right well resembles;
> The other his pale cheeks, methinks,
>     presenteth.
> Wither one rose, and let the other flourish.
> If you contend, a thousand lives must wither.
> (II, v, 94–102)

Henry's sorrow is deep and real. He is the one figure of compassion in a brutal world, where all the others stand for unremitting vengeance. He is a man of goodwill, demonstrably ineffective except when he is allied with men who stand for social order—Lord Talbot in the first play, Humphrey Duke of Gloucester in the second.

In contrast with the king are virtually all the other characters, who in one way or another are representatives of rampant egoism, which disrupts order and ultimately leads to a breakdown of society. In this play, the prime exemplar that emerges is York's son Richard, who has his own play, *Richard III*. But the groundwork for his characterization is provided in *3 Henry VI*. He is the ultimate predator, the logical culmination in the process of disorder. The motives of the others are understandable; they come from the heart, however imperfect it may be. Richard is inhuman. His acts are motivated by will, a deliberate stretching of volitional curiosity as to what it is possible to achieve if all moral limits are pushed aside.

We get a sharply etched portrait of him from his long soliloquy in III, ii. Speaking of his brother, King Edward IV, he declares:

> Would he were wasted, marrow, bones, and all,
> That from his loins no hopeful branch may
> spring
> To cross me from the golden time I look for.
> And yet, between my soul's desire and me—
> The lustful Edward's title buried—
> Is Clarence, Henry, and his son young Edward,
> And all the unlooked-for issue of their bodies,
> To take their rooms ere I can place myself.
>
> (III, ii, 125–32)

Looking at his misshapen body, Richard can see no other pleasure for himself than forwarding his ambition and he vows

> I'll make my heaven to dream upon the crown
> And, whiles I live, t'account this world but hell
> Until my misshaped trunk that bears this head
> Be round impaled with a glorious crown.
>
> (III, ii, 168–71)

Therefore he determines on a course of duplicity:

> Why, I can smile, and murder whiles I smile,
> And cry 'Content!' to that which grieves my
>   heart,
> And wet my cheeks with artificial tears,
> And frame my face to all occasions . . .
> I can add colors to the chameleon,
> Change shapes with Proteus for advantages,
> And set the murderous Machiavel to school.
>
> (III, ii, 182–85; 191–93)

That is, he will outdo Machiavelli, who to the Elizabethans was the archetype of murderous duplicity.

Henry VI and Richard are contrasted in character in the final episode of the play. Henry, who has been temporarily restored as king, hands over his rule to Warwick and Clarence, with the intention of leading a private life and of spending his latter days in prayer. Richard urges his returning brother Edward to seize the throne again, for "fearless minds climb soonest unto crowns." In the battle at Tewkesbury, Warwick and his brother, Montague, are killed; Queen Margaret, the Prince of Wales, the Earl of Oxford, and the Duke of Somerset are captured. Oxford is imprisoned, Somerset beheaded. The prince, brought before his

captors, taunts them as his mother had previously
taunted York:

> Lascivious Edward, and thou perjured George,
> And thou misshapen Dick, I tell ye all
> I am your better, traitors as ye are,
> And thou usurp'st my father's right and mine.
> (V, v, 34–37)

Without delay Edward IV, Richard, and Clarence stab
the youth in turn. Richard is ready to kill Queen Margaret too, but Edward IV restrains him. Then Richard
runs off stage, muttering "The Tower, the Tower."

In the Tower, Henry VI is well aware what Richard's appearance portends. The ex-king, mild as he is,
shows a considerable talent for invective, prophesying

>             that many a thousand
> Which now mistrust no parcel of my fear,
> And many an old man's sigh and many a
>     widow's,
> And many an orphan's water-standing eye—
> Men for their sons, wives for their husbands,
> Orphans for their parents' timeless death—
> Shall rue the hour that ever thou wast born.
> (V, vi, 37–43)

Richard stabs Henry. Not content with one blow, he
stabs again after Henry dies, saying

> Down, down to hell, and say I sent thee thither.
> (V, vi, 67)

He immediately looks forward to his next bloody step
to the throne:

> King Henry and the prince his son are gone.
> Clarence, thy turn is next, and then the rest,
> Counting myself but bad till I be best.
>
> (V, vi, 89–91)

With the murder of saintly Henry, Richard, a diabolical force, has come into his own.

Lacking formal coherence, the three Henry VI plays—Shakespeare's first essays in the historical genre —impose themselves upon the audience by reiterated visual and verbal impact. They are not subtle; they make no effort to develop character beyond stereotype; they have the obviousness of the morality play. But they do provide an unrelenting picture of horror born of ambition, treachery, and rampant egoism. In their very confusion these plays convey the social chaos that attends civil war.

To the knowledgeable Elizabethan, they conveyed more than that. The fratricidal frenzy of the Wars of the Roses was the next to final step in a providential progress brought about by the forced abdication of Richard II, a divine retribution prophesied by the Bishop of Carlisle at the time of Richard's fall. The line of usurping Henry of Lancaster had been extinguished. But it was also part of God's plan to punish the contentious house of York and to extinguish it also, in preparation for the reconciliation of the Tudor king, Henry VII.

## The Life and Death of
## Richard the Third

As drama *Richard III* is everything that the
Henry VI plays are not. It is unified, coherent, and dy-
namic. Part of the reason for this is the masterly compression of events running over a span of fourteen years
into what appears to be a single continuous action.

In terms of actual history, the play begins with the
funeral of Henry VI, which took place on May 23,
1471. The next significant event is the murder of
George Duke of Clarence, the brother of Edward IV
and Richard III, occurring on February 18, 1478. This
is followed by the death of Edward IV on April 9,
1483. In the play these events seem to follow immediately one on the other.

Similarly, after Richard III becomes king on June
26, 1483, the two years of his reign are so telescoped
that an abortive insurrection led by the Duke of Buckingham in October 1483 seems to be followed immediately by the invasion of the Earl of Richmond, Henry
Tudor, and the battle at Bosworth Field (August 22,
1485), at which Richard III was killed and Richmond
ascended the throne as Henry VII.

Numerous as the characters are, they are fairly well

differentiated. What the spectator has to bear in mind is that the House of Lancaster, of which Henry VI was the last king, has come to an end. Only Lady Anne, the widow of the Lancastrian Prince of Wales, and Dowager Queen Margaret, widow of Henry VI, are left as representatives of the former ruling house. (Margaret's presence is completely unhistorical, since she returned to France in 1475 and died in 1482.) The Yorkist faction is represented by Edward IV, George Duke of Clarence, and Richard Duke of Gloucester, the three sons of the late Duke of York, and by the offspring of the two older brothers, in particular the two young sons of Edward IV, who were incarcerated in the Tower of London in 1483 and never seen again.

An important group within the Yorkist dynasty are Queen Elizabeth and her family, the Woodvilles, who, as soon as she became Edward IV's queen, clamored for and received high place in the kingdom. At Edward's death, Anthony Woodville, Earl Rivers, the queen's brother, and the Marquess of Dorset and Lord Grey, her sons by her first marriage, were in jeopardy from Richard III and his supporters, who had been jealous of these upstarts' sudden rise to power.

Four additional personalities have important roles in the play. Henry Tudor, the Earl of Richmond, was claimant to the throne by default after the male Yorkists and Lancastrians had been killed off. He was a Lancastrian by descent through the female line from the Beauforts, John of Gaunt's second (and illegitimate) family. Henry's mother was married to Thomas Lord Stanley, who played an ambiguous role in the politics of the time. Ostensibly a supporter of Richard III, Stanley withheld his military support at a critical moment, insuring Richard's defeat at Bosworth Field. In gratitude, Henry VII created him Earl of Derby as one of the first acts of his reign.

Lord Hastings, Lord Chamberlain under Edward IV, was another well-defined personality. There was implacable hatred between him and Queen Elizabeth. Thus he was a willing adherent of Richard III until the latter tried to enlist his approval of the murder of Edward IV's sons. Richard promptly accused him of a treasonous plot and had him beheaded. The plight of Henry Stafford, second Duke of Buckingham, was much the same. He went along with Richard III in his designs on the crown, but broke with him when not suitably rewarded for his assistance, mounted an insurrection in favor of Henry Tudor, and was captured and beheaded.

Finally, Richard Duke of Gloucester, who allegedly murdered his two nephews and who ruled for two years as Richard III, was according to sixteenth-century historians a monster. Holinshed, incorporating Sir Thomas More's account, describes him thus:

> Richard . . . was in wit and courage equal with either of them [Edward IV and the Duke of Clarence], in body and prowess far under them both; little of stature, ill-featured of limbs, crook backed, his left shoulder much higher than his right, hard favored of visage . . . he was malicious, wrathful, envious, and from before his birth ever froward. . . . He was close and secret, a deep dissembler, lowly of countenance, arrogant of heart, outwardly companionable where he inwardly hated, not letting [hesitating] to kiss whom he thought to kill; despitious and cruel, not for evil will always, but ofter for ambition, and either for the surety or increase of his estate. Friend and foe was much what indifferent, where his advantage grew; he spared no man's death whose life withstood his purpose. . . . I have heard by credible report of such as were secret with his chamberlain,

> that, after this abominable deed done [the murder
> of the princes], he never had a quiet mind. . . .
> Where he went abroad, his eyes whirled about, his
> body privily fenced, his hand ever upon his dag-
> ger, his countenance and manner like one always
> ready to strike again; he took ill rest of nights, lay
> long waking and musing, sore wearied with care
> and watch, rather slumbered than slept, troubled
> with fearful dreams, suddenly sometimes started
> up, leapt out of bed, and ran about the chamber. . . .

Shakespeare does not change the outlines of this
portrait, though he does refine and embellish them. He
gives us the monster live, so to speak, never allowing
us to forget Richard, even when he is offstage. The
play's coherence comes from the primacy Richard receives. To a degree that is unusual before the great
tragedies, this is *his* play. Richard is a two-dimensional
stereotype—the "heavy" that we find in all conventional melodrama—who here takes on life and substance by the generation of incredible energy. His two
opening soliloquies tell us bluntly what he is and what
he is going to do. The play is the fleshing out of that
announced program. Then we witness the consequences, which Richard did not envisage and which
we as audience fear may not befall him, so diabolically
powerful he seems to be.

As Richard appears on stage alone, he muses on his
situation now that the House of York has finally disposed of Lancaster:

> Now is the winter of our discontent
> Made glorious summer by this son of York;
> And all the clouds that lowered upon our house
> In the deep bosom of the ocean buried.
>
> (I, i, 1–4)

War is over and his brother King Edward is capering "nimbly in a lady's chamber to the lascivious pleasing of a lute."

> But I, that am not shaped for sportive tricks
> Nor made to court an amorous looking-glass;
> I, that am rudely stamped, and want love's
>     majesty
> To strut before a wanton ambling nymph;
> I, that am curtailed of this fair proportion,
> Cheated of feature by dissembling Nature,
> Deformed, unfinished, sent before my time
> Into this breathing world, scarce half made up,
> And that so lamely and unfashionable
> That dogs bark at me as I halt by them . . .
> And therefore, since I cannot prove a lover
> To entertain these fair well-spoken days,
> I am determined to prove a villain
> And hate the idle pleasures of these days.
>              (I, i, 14–23, 28–31)

Richard tells us that he has set in motion a plot to turn his brother Edward against his brother Clarence. When he talks to Clarence, however, he assures his brother that he is doing everything in his power to release him from prison. Then encountering Lord Hastings, he learns of the dangerous illness of Edward. Richard's nimble mind immediately weighs the possibilities of the situation:

> He cannot live, I hope, and must not die
> Till George be packed with posthorse up to
>     heaven.
> I'll in, to urge his hatred more to Clarence
> With lies well steeled with weighty arguments;
> And, if I fail not in my deep intent,
> Clarence hath not another day to live:

> Which done, God take King Edward to his
>     mercy
> And leave the world for me to bustle in!
>
> (I, i, 145–52)

His next step will be to marry Lady Anne, in spite of
the fact that he has killed her husband (the Prince of
Wales) and her father (Warwick). However, he must
not "run before my horse to market":

> Clarence still breathes; Edward still lives and
>     reigns;
> When they are gone, then must I count my
>     gains.
>
> (I, i, 161–62)

In describing his physical deformity Richard is not
playing for sympathy or providing psychological ex-
planation for his rancor. Rather, he is glorying in his
difference from others and setting himself a challenge
to see what he can do with such outwardly unpromis-
ing material. He is "determined to prove a villain" and
by being "subtle, false and treacherous" to disturb social and moral order. He needs unlimited room "to
bustle in." In other words, the kingship that he seeks is
only part of his goal. Rather, it is action for its own
sake that interests him, in the same way that for Iago
in *Othello* pleasure in action makes the hours seem
short. Richard revels in evildoing, even more in cloak-
ing his evil purposes in the appearance of virtue, seeming a saint when most he plays the devil. He enjoys
role-playing, and it is a conscious role-playing. He
hides nothing from himself or the audience. In fact, it
is the complicity developed between Richard and the
audience that gives the play its special zest.

Richard's first encounter—with Lady Anne as she

accompanies the coffin of Henry VI—is a virtuoso performance. Her lament for fallen Lancaster turns to vituperation as she attempts to exorcise Richard as the devil:

> Avaunt, thou dreadful minister of hell!
> Thou hadst but power over his mortal body;
> His soul thou canst not have. Therefore, be
>     gone.
>
> (I, ii, 46–48)

In 200 lines of spirited dialogue he brings her around to tentative acceptance of his proposal of marriage. Richard is beside himself with glee:

> Was ever woman in this humor wooed?
> Was ever woman in this humor won?
> I'll have her, but I will not keep her long.
> What? I that killed her husband and his father
> To take her in her heart's extremest hate,
> With curses in her mouth, tears in her eyes. . . .
>
> (I, ii, 227–32)

He is convinced that he can fail at nothing.

This success is followed by the murder of the Duke of Clarence, of which we have already been forewarned. Clarence, rather belatedly concerned for his immortal soul, pleads with the two executioners. He tells them that his brother Richard will reward them better for saving his life than King Edward will for killing him. Finally, Clarence receives the revelation that it is Richard who has sent the murderers to him. The closest bonds of fraternal love and trust have been broken. Richard compounds his duplicity by assuming innocence before the king and court and placing the guilt on the Queen Elizabeth's adherents.

While Richard is not instrumental in Edward IV's death, he takes quick advantage of it to remove the legitimate heirs and to destroy the queen's party. Earl Rivers, Lord Grey, and Sir Thomas Vaughan are intercepted on their way to London with young Edward V and are hustled off to execution at Pontrefact —the ill-omened castle where Richard II was murdered eighty-four years before. Hearing of this, the queen wisely seeks sanctuary in the Abbey of Westminster with her younger son, then unwisely yields the boy up to Richard. Both princes are lodged in the Tower of London, ostensibly in preparation for the coronation of Edward V. Richard sets a plot in motion to secure the crown for himself. Here his role-playing reaches its skilled and sinister peak.

At a meeting of the royal council, Lord Hastings, who had shown horror at the idea of passing over Edward IV's son, observes fatuously of Richard that there is no man in Christendom less able to hide his hate or love than he. At that moment Richard strides angrily in, charges Hastings with a plot against his life, and declares:

> Thou art a traitor.
> Off with his head! Now by Saint Paul I swear
> I will not dine until I see the same.
>
> (III, iv, 75–77)

Two scenes later we learn that the indictment against Hastings had been prepared hours before the sudden discovery of his treason. So much for Richard's spontaneous outrage!

Buckingham becomes Richard's stage manager in the next set of maneuvers as he has been his eager follower in the earlier ones. He is to start a rumor about the illegitimacy of Edward IV's children and even to touch on the fact that Edward himself could not have been the son of the Duke of York. Buckingham's attempts to rouse the citizenry into acclamation of Richard as king fall flat, to Richard's disgust. He stages a new show, standing aloft between two holy bishops, when the Lord Mayor comes at Buckingham's urging to ask him to assume the throne. Richard at last gives in, allowing a sense of duty to overcome his reluctance. In a fine show of humility, he addresses the mayor, aldermen, and citizens:

> Since you will buckle fortune on my back,
> To bear her burden, wh'er I will or no,
> I must have patience to endure the load;
> But if black scandal or foul-faced reproach
> Attend the sequel of your imposition,
> Your mere enforcement shall acquittance me
> From all the impure blots and stains thereof;
> For God doth know, and you may partly see,
> How far I am from the desire of this.
>
> (III, vii, 228–36)

One step remains. Richard must dispose of the two princes. He sounds out Buckingham on this, but "high-reaching Buckingham grows circumspect." Richard learns in the same scene that the Marquess of Dorset, the queen's son, has joined Henry Tudor, the Earl of Richmond, in Brittany. Richard's response is not one of panic but of quick and effective calculation. He sees no danger from Clarence's simple son; he will marry Clarence's daughter off to some mean-born gentleman. He will dispose of his wife Queen Anne and then marry Elizabeth (his niece, Edward IV's daughter) to consolidate his position. And he finds an ambitious hanger-on at court, Sir James Tyrrel, to murder the princes. Unemotionally, Richard concludes:

> I must be married to my brother's daughter,
> Or else my kingdom stands on brittle glass:
> Murder her brothers, and then marry her—
> Uncertain way of gain! But I am in
> So far in blood that sin will pluck on sin.
> Tear-falling pity dwells not in this eye.
>
> (IV, ii, 59–64)

At this point in his career the gusto begins to disappear. Richard on the defensive is less attractive, as becomes apparent in three conversations. He demeans himself by direct contact with Tyrrel. Then, worrying about Richmond, he is almost petulant that he had not earlier been informed of the fortunate destiny prophesied by Henry VI (*3 Henry VI*, IV, vi, 68 ff) so that he might have disposed of Richmond while he had the chance. Finally, he insolently ignores Buckingham's equally insolent demand for the reward he had been promised. We see a new Richard, whose egoism is without charm, whose brutality no amount of casuistry can conceal.

The decline in Richard's exuberance is marked by the scene with Queen Elizabeth in which he seeks the hand of her daughter, Elizabeth (IV, iv). This parallels the early scene in which he successfully woos Lady Anne. For a moment his spirits revive as he contemplates becoming once more "a jolly thriving wooer." But his suit is perfunctory, the outcome is uncertain, and his summing up is curt and preoccupied:

> Relenting fool, and shallow, changing woman!
>
> (IV, iv, 431)

In the period preceding the final battle, except for one outburst of temper, Richard is almost stoic as he faces disaster:

I have not that alacrity of spirit
Nor cheer of mind that I was wont to have.
(V, iii, 73–74)

His last words before the battle are resigned:

I have set my life upon a cast,
And I will stand the hazard of the die.
(V, iv, 9–10)

This is in contrast with the exhilaration with which he has met earlier challenges.

The most critical speech for evaluation of his personality is the one that follows his dream in V, iii. In a highly ritual scene, the ghosts of all Richard's victims appear first to Richard, then to Richmond, threatening disaster and condign punishment to the one, predicting victory for the other. As Richard starts into consciousness, he is terrified and cries "Have mercy, Jesu!," a most uncharacteristic show of weakness for him.

Then his rationality takes over. He admits that he is afflicted by "coward conscience" and that he is a murderer and a perjurer in direst degree. He accepts the fact that no one loves him or will pity him after his death. This acceptance is not the cry of a soul in despair, merely a matter-of-fact balancing of moral accounts. It is not recognition by a great but imperfect hero that he should have been better. It is a coldly rational self-examination, in which egoism, the assertion that "I am I," persists to the grave.

The astonishing thing about this play is that until almost the end there is no sign of a possible antagonist, no visible secular force that can bring the tyrant down. Richmond is not even mentioned until Act IV, and appears in only the last three scenes. He is little more than a *deus ex machina* let down from above to provide a resolution both for the immediate action of this play and for the long-continued drama of conflict between York and Lancaster.

For two actions go on simultaneously in *Richard III*. The primary one is the rise and fall of an evil man, a demi-devil. The second is the working out, the purging, of the evil force let loose almost a century before by the forced abdication and eventual murder of Richard II. These two actions are reasonably congruent. Richard III is not only an evil man; he is also the fated final term in a series of evil men and women who have brought England to disaster, who have dissolved the bonds of natural order. Thus he is a scapegoat offered up for the appeasement of divine wrath.

It is this double format that dictates the delayed appearance of and relative unimportance of Richmond. He is merely God's instrument in the resolution of both actions. As the leader under whose aegis Richard is brought down, we do not need to be told how he reached that position or what claim he had to the crown. It is necessary merely that he personally kill Richard and close the play with a speech of reconciliation.

This double format also explains the presence of Queen Margaret, Henry VI's widow, a presence that is paradoxical as well as unhistorical. This "she-wolf of France" has been the embodiment of Lancastrian ferocity in the civil war, in her way as much of a monster as Richard himself and therefore deserving of the same annihilation as he. Yet in this play she stands as a figure of nemesis. It is the justice and ineluctability of her curses that the various characters—Rivers, Grey, and Vaughan; Hastings and Buckingham— acknowledge as one by one they fall to death.

Queen Margaret's function is more than that of simple chorus lamenting past wrongs and putting them in perspective. She is the nucleus of a sense of moral outrage that will bring Richard down, a force feeble and personally vindictive in the beginning, but one that grows in power as victim after victim adds his tale of woe. In default of a visible antagonist it is this sense of outrage that will weigh in the scales against the apparently invincible tyrant, very much in the way that the anguish of suffering Scotland weighs against the tyrant Macbeth. Moral disorder cannot be permanent. By its reckless cancerous growth it insures its own destruction.

The choric cursing and lamentation of which Queen Margaret becomes the symbol appears in the second scene, where Lady Anne calls Richard a devil and utters the first curse—apparently ineffective since she immediately succumbs to Richard's snares and wiles. In the next scene, in the midst of a quarrel between Queen Elizabeth and Richard, Elizabeth complains

Small joy have I in being England's queen.

To this Margaret, unseen in the shadows, makes choric response. Then, unable to contain her satisfaction, she comes forward and confronts the quarreling Yorkists, calling them

wrangling pirates, that fall out
In sharing that which you have pilled from
me!
(I, iii, 157–58)

She rehearses the wrongs done her and her family and prays God

That none of you may live his natural age,
But by some unlooked accident cut off!
(I, iii, 212–13)

She prophesies that each of them will live subject to Richard's hate, and he to theirs, and all of them to God's (I, iii, 301–02).

As the horrors attendant on Richard's wading through slaughter to the throne increase, there are more passages of lamentation, particularly after the death of King Edward (II, ii, 34–88) and after news is received of the capture of Rivers, Grey, and Vaughan (II, iv, 49–65). In each case Queen Elizabeth is joined in grief and dire foreboding by the Dowager Duchess of York, who has lost three of her four sons. That family, recently prospering, now has its share of woe.

These passages are preparatory to the Dowager Queen Margaret's reappearance in IV, iv, which is the key scene of the play. Still vindictive, still gleeful as she listens to the Dowager Queen Elizabeth and the Dowager Duchess recite their litany of loss, she comes forward to join them. Admitting that she has been hungry for revenge but is now cloyed with beholding it, she directs all her wrath at Richard, calling him "hell's black intelligencer." However, she foresees

> his piteous and unpitied end.
> Earth gapes, hell burns, fiends roar, saints pray,
> To have him suddenly conveyed from hence.
> Cancel his bond of life, dear God, I pray,
> That I may live and say, "The dog is dead."
> (IV, iv, 74–78)

Then, in the favorite medieval mode of an *Ubi sunt* (a listing of those dead and gone by repeating the question "Where is ——?"), Margaret calls the roll of Elizabeth's sorrows, though still giving her own grief primacy. She leaves the burden of cursing and sorrow to Elizabeth and the Dowager Duchess. If not united, the women of Lancaster and York have reached an equality of grief, and they are at one in calling down God's wrath on Richard, the duchess even wishing that she had strangled him "in her accursed womb." Such a concert of lamentation and revulsion cannot fail to rise to heaven and bring down divine punishment.

Because of its formal rhetoric and its high-flown, artificial language, this scene is almost impossible to play without its descending to the ridiculous. Yet by separating the scene from the flow of action, this rhetoric gives it weight and demands full realization of the gravity of the underlying issue. To omit Margaret, as many productions have done, is to destroy the play as written, reducing it to mere melodrama—a safely vicarious romp with the devil almost casually capped by a moral ending. *Richard III* is certainly a history play; it makes use of the monster that Sir Thomas More created; it pays pious, though brief, tribute to the unification of interest and the conciliation of faction on which the Tudors preened themselves.

But it is much more than that. It is a sophisticated morality play, utilizing real people and real situations from history to assert that however undecipherable God's purposes may be, they mean good, and that ultimately good triumphs at however great a cost. This is *histoire moralisée*: Meaning takes precedence over action, but the action is substantial and dramatic in a way that the action in the old conventional morality plays never was.

## The Life of
## King Henry the Eighth

The simplest way to describe *King Henry VIII* is as a loosely strung together chronicle providing a framework of spectacle of a lavishness not unlike that of a court masque. In Arthur Quiller-Couch's phrase, it is "a procession in tapestry." It is likely that this scenic aspect of the play is due to a ceremonial purpose. King James I's daughter Elizabeth was married to a German princeling, the Elector Palatine, on February 14, 1613.* Shakespeare's company honored the event by putting on "fowerteene severall playes," of which six were by Shakespeare. *Henry VIII* is not listed by name, but it is certainly similar to other entertainments of masquelike format that were put together for the occasion, and it was still considered a new play when it was publicly performed at the Globe Theater in June 1613. Both the praise bestowed on Queen Elizabeth and the implicit Protestantism of the play would have made it inherently suitable as a compliment to Princess Eliza-

---

* It is from this marriage that George I, the first Hanoverian king, traced his descent and his right to the crown when Queen Anne, the last of the Stuarts, died in 1714.

beth Stuart and her consort, a leader of the German Protestants.

Basically, the play encompasses events extending from what we would call a summit meeting of the kings of England and France at the so-called Field of the Cloth of Gold in Flanders in June 1520 to the christening of Henry VIII's daughter Elizabeth in 1533. However, it also covers the death of Queen Katherine on January 7, 1536, and a plot against Thomas Cranmer, the Archbishop of Canterbury, in 1544.

The play is made up of six major dramatic incidents: 1) the trial and execution of Edward Stafford, third Duke of Buckingham, for treason in May 1521; 2) Henry VIII's repudiation of Queen Katherine in favor of Anne Boleyn, a political and legal maneuver that took six years, from 1527 to 1533; 3) Anne Boleyn's coronation as queen on June 1, 1533; 4) the disgrace and death of Cardinal Wolsey in 1529 and 1530; 5) the plot against Archbishop Cranmer in 1544; 6) the christening of Princess Elizabeth Tudor on September 13, 1533.

There is no logical progression in these events. Some of them merely serve as occasions for spectacle. All of them exhibit major personalities of the times, whose names and fates were part of the national legend.

The fall of Edward Stafford, third Duke of Buckingham, forms a kind of curtain raiser to the main action of the play. The Staffords were descended from Thomas, first Duke of Gloucester, Edward III's sixth son. They were arrogantly conscious of their royal ancestry, and in the free-for-all of the Wars of the Roses in the fifteenth century they came to feel that their claim on the throne was as good as anyone else's. The second duke rebelled against Richard III and was beheaded, with his descendants under attainder. That is, their titles and rights were annulled by the king. Henry VII restored those rights, even though thereby he granted status to a dangerous rival. It could, in fact, be argued that the Stafford claim was better than that of the Tudors, whose descent involved a double bastardy.

At any rate, what we see at the beginning of *Henry VIII* is a Duke of Buckingham restive under what he considers the ruthless exercise of power of the king's chancellor, Cardinal Wolsey. The hatred of Buckingham for Wolsey is quickly established in the opening scene. Buckingham declares to the Duke of Norfolk, another powerful and ambitious noble, that

> No man's pie is freed
> From his [Wolsey's] ambitious finger.
> (I, i, 52–53)

Norfolk warns Buckingham to be cautious in his remarks about Wolsey because "the state takes notice of the private difference" between them. At this moment Wolsey and his retinue pass across the stage. He and Buckingham glare at each other. Buckingham is disturbed:

> This butcher's cur is venom-mouthed, and I
> Have not the power to muzzle him; therefore best
> Not wake him in his slumber. A beggar's book
> Outworths a noble's blood.
> (I, i, 120–23)

This resolution is too late. Buckingham is arrested for high treason and hauled off to the Tower.

Three scenes later, Buckingham, having been con-

victed by the perjured testimony of a dismissed ser-
vant, appears on his way to execution. With unexpected, and uncharacteristic, piety and humility, he
asserts his loyalty to the king, forgives his enemies,
and commends himself to God. The audience has an
emphatic vision of this noble man as a victim of Cardinal Wolsey's efficient malevolence.

The main conflict of the play has already been
joined in I, ii, a scene where King Henry, Queen
Katherine, and Cardinal Wolsey are all present at a
meeting held to discuss Buckingham's treason. The
king is grateful to Wolsey for unmasking the plot.
The queen unexpectedly brings up the heavy taxation
imposed by Wolsey that has caused the weavers to
revolt. When Wolsey attempts to evade responsibility,
Katherine sharply calls him to task. The upshot is that
she forces him to back down, though Wolsey manages
to make it appear that it is his intercession that has
brought about the revocation of the taxes he himself
had imposed. Katherine is less successful in interceding
for Buckingham, though she does point out that Buckingham's chief accuser's evidence is suspect.

Insofar as the play has a dramatic center, it is in the
conflict between Katherine and Wolsey, and in the
contrast of their personalities. Katherine on her first
appearance is established as the epitome of womanly,
and queenly, self-abnegation and compassion, in contrast to Wolsey's arrogant self-seeking. The audience
is on her side from the beginning. Rigging of historical
fact insures that their fates shall appear to be parallel,
since Katherine learns of Wolsey's death as she is
about to die. (In fact, Wolsey died in 1530, Katherine
in 1536, outside the time span of the play.)

In the scene described above, Henry and Katherine
seem to be living and ruling in loving amity. Yet almost immediately we see Henry smitten with the

charms of Anne Boleyn, a maid of honor to the queen. This infatuation provokes his determination to secure a divorce, though in the play and in fact he cloaked his motives in religious scruples. Katherine had originally been married to Prince Arthur, Henry's older brother, and had come to England in 1503 as his bride. After the prince's death it was considered desirable to continue the Spanish alliance by marrying her to Henry. It was this union with his deceased brother's widow about which the king raised convenient scruples twenty years later. Henry sought to secure a divorce, or rather an annulment, from the Pope. The Pope was not eager to affront Charles V, the Holy Roman Emperor and king of Spain, who was Katherine's nephew. Wolsey's role was ambiguous. On the one hand, he was ambitious to be elected pope himself; on the other, he hated Charles V and wanted to ingratiate himself further with Henry.

There was long delay. The Pope sent Cardinal Campeius to hold a trial of the case along with Wolsey. Eventually, when the delay became unbearable to Henry VIII, he solved his difficulty by having Archbishop Cranmer influence English clerics to approve the annulment. This flouting of papal authority in turn led to the establishment of the Church of England with Henry as supreme head. The Reformation in England was more political than doctrinal, in its origins.

Queen Katherine and Cardinal Wolsey are antagonists in two powerful scenes. The first (II, iv) opens with a lavish ceremonial procession of the king, queen, churchmen, and nobles who will participate in Katherine's trial. Summoned to the bar of justice, Katherine kneels at Henry's feet, pleading that she has been faithful and dutiful. She questions the fairness of the trial:

I am a most poor woman and a stranger,
Born out of your dominions: having here
No judge indifferent, nor no more assurance
Of equal friendship and proceeding.

(II, iv, 13–16)

She denies that the marriage to Henry was invalid
because of her previous union with Prince Arthur:

                    Please you, sir,
The king your father was reputed for
A prince most prudent, of an excellent
And unmatched wit and judgment. Ferdinand,
My father, King of Spain, was reckoned one
The wisest prince that there had reigned by
        many
A year before. It is not to be questioned that
They had gathered a wise council to them
Of every realm, that did debate this business,
Who deemed our marriage lawful.

(II, iv, 42–51)

Katherine asks for delay in the proceedings until she
can consult her friends in Spain. The cardinals will
admit of no delay. From pleading, Katherine turns to
accusation. Addressing Wolsey, she bursts out:

I am about to weep; but, thinking that
We were a queen (or long have dreamed so),
        certain
The daughter of a king, my drops of tears
I'll turn to sparks of fire.

(II, iv, 68–71)

To Wolsey's counsel of patience, she replies:

I will, when you are humble; nay before,
Or God will punish me. I do believe

> (Induced by potent circumstances) that
> You are mine enemy; and make my challenge
> You shall not be my judge. For it is you
> Have blown this coal betwixt my lord and
>      me—
> Which God's dew quench! Therefore I say
>      again
> I utterly abhor, yea, from my soul
> Refuse you for my judge, whom yet once more
> I hold my most malicious foe and think not
> At all a friend to truth.
>
> (II, iv, 72–82)

To Wolsey's denial of any responsibility for the divorce, Katherine rejoins that he is cunning, and that his heart is "crammed with arrogancy, spleen, and pride":

> I do refuse you for my judge and here,
> Before you all, appeal unto the pope. . . .
>
> (II, iv, 116–17)

She sweeps out of the court and refuses to come back.

In the following scene the two cardinals attempt in private to sway the queen to obedience to Henry's wishes. Again, Katherine is enraged by their smooth words and pious attitudes:

> Holy men I thought ye,
> Upon my soul, two reverent cardinal virtues;
> But cardinal sins and hollow hearts I fear ye:
>
> (III, i, 104–06)

Declaring that "nothing but death shall e'er divorce my dignities," she bewails her exiled state:

> Would I had never trod this English earth
> Or felt the flatteries that grow upon it!

Ye have angels' faces, but heaven knows your
    hearts.
What will become of me now, wretched lady?
I am the most unhappy woman living.

Then addressing her ladies-in-waiting:

Alas, poor wenches, where are now your
    fortunes?
Shipwracked upon a kingdom where no pity,
No friends, no hope, no kindred weep for me,
Almost no grave allowed me. Like the lily
That once was mistress of the field and
    flourished,
I'll hang my head and perish.

                            (III, i, 143–53)

Suddenly she loses heart, apologizes to the cardinals
for her unmannerly behavior, and asks their counsel.

We see Katherine, now Princess Dowager, once
more. She is ill and resigned to her fate. For a moment,
her spirit flares up as she hears of the death of Wolsey,
who, she says, "was a man of an unbounded stomach,
ever ranking himself with princes; one that by suggestion tied all the kingdom." Lord Capuchius comes to
her bearing Henry's "princely commendations."
Katherine sends back to Henry a letter in which she
begs his consideration for their daughter Mary and for
her ladies-in-waiting, now cast adrift in a foreign land.
Knowing that she is about to die, Katherine tells
Capuchius to

                    Remember me
In all humility unto his highness.
Say his long trouble now is passing
Out of this world. Tell him in death I blessed
    him,
For so I will.

                            (IV, ii, 160–64)

Queen Katherine's unprepared-for transition from spiritedness to meekness is paralleled by a like transformation in the character of Cardinal Wolsey. By the testimony of others and by his own actions he early appears to be an almost diabolic figure. He is spiderlike, revengeful, corrupt, and treasonous. Buckingham says that Wolsey buys and sells King Henry's honor as he pleases. It is suggested that he is responsible for the king's sudden scruples about the marriage. He acts the "king-cardinal" and in his greed will eat up all the kingdom. He sees to it that possible rivals are kept out of the king's sight. Courtiers look on aghast and vacillate between sycophancy and the hope that one day the king will know "this bold bad man" for what he is.

After such a build-up, the audience takes great satisfaction in the climactic scene in which King Henry, having at last seen through Wolsey, leads him on to more and more fulsome protestations of virtue and loyalty, and then destroys his pretense by handing him a misplaced inventory, in which Wolsey has listed his corruptly accumulated wealth. The king ends with the ironical suggestion that Wolsey go "to breakfast with what appetite you have" (III, ii, 202–03).

When various nobles come to reclaim the great seal —the insignium of the chancellor's office—Wolsey shows himself in his true visage, a wolf-cardinal snarling and at bay, threatening reprisal, until he is overwhelmed by the weight of the charges against him. Then in a sudden and unbelievable volteface, he in soliloquy and in conversation with Cromwell, his secretary, admits his error and casts all vanity from him:

> Had I but served my God with half the zeal
> I served my king, he would not in mine age
> Have left me naked to mine enemies.
>
> (III, ii, 455–57)

Anne Boleyn, the not so innocent cause of Queen Katherine's rejection, appears in only three scenes. First, there is the banquet at Cardinal Wolsey's palace (I, iv), at which the king and others enter as "maskers, habited like shepherds," choose partners among the assembled ladies, and form a stately dance, as a prelude to the king's discovery of Anne Boleyn's charms. Anne, who has had a flirtatious exchange with one of the courtiers early in the scene, says not a word to Henry. Second, in IV, i, there is Anne's coronation as Henry's second queen. Her role here is that of a mute vision of loveliness as the most elaborate procession in all of Shakespeare passes over the stage. In between these two spectacles, there is a short scene (II, iii) in which she is presented as modest, humble, unambitious, and deeply concerned over the fate of Queen Katherine.

King Henry VIII is present in all parts of the play as the common factor in the successive episodes. Yet of the English kings whom Shakespeare represents, he is the least interesting because the least defined. His role is merely reactive. He has no depth, or rather his depth is never probed. We do not know what his real feelings are toward Katherine. He masks any disappointment he may feel over the birth of a daughter to Queen Anne. Rapacity, lechery, hypocrisy, and unbridled will there may be beneath his stately seeming, but the play does not permit these traits to be brought out. He is the charming golden prince of the early years of his reign, not the gross caricature of a king portrayed by Charles Laughton in the film.

Henry's role is particularly ambiguous in relation to Archbishop Cranmer, whose near escape from disgrace provides the next to last episode of the play. Cranmer is first mentioned in III, ii as "A worthy fellow" about to be made archbishop in reward for the much pain he has taken in the business of the divorce.

Then in the last act we see Cranmer under attack by Stephen Gardiner, Bishop of Winchester, for heretical Lutheran sympathies. The king, forewarned of the attack on the archbishop, allows the plot to go forward, intervening at the last moment as a *deus ex machina* to put Cranmer's adversaries to rout.

Then without transition the play ends in another spectacle, that of the christening of the future Queen Elizabeth I, at which Cranmer prophesies a golden age for England when the infant princess becomes queen.

All these bits and pieces of dramatic action are framed in spectacle, but the latter cannot fully conceal the play's basic incoherence. We are left to find in it as best we can some unified impression, some coherent image of historical truth underlying the disparate elements of which it is made up. If such order exists, it is to be found in the commonplace Elizabethan interest in the fall of princes. The Prologue, full of conventional sententious observations, concludes with this theme: The play will not evoke laughter; it is "full of state and woe":

> Think ye see
> The very persons of our noble story
> As they were living. Think you see them great,
> And followed with the general throng and
> sweat
> Of thousand friends. Then, in a moment, see
> How soon this mightiness meets misery.
>
> (25–30)

In *Henry VIII*, as we have already seen, three major descents from mightiness to misery are set before the audience, that of Wolsey, fully merited; that of Buckingham, ambiguous as to desert; and that of Queen Katherine, completely undeserved. Each fall comes suddenly and unexpectedly when fortune seems to be at its peak. Each is marked by insistent rhetorical flourish. The play opens with Buckingham's being told that by his absence from the Field of the Cloth of Gold he "lost the view of earthly glory" provided there. Two hundred lines later Buckingham has been arrested and is lamenting

> my life is spanned already.
> I am the shadow of poor Buckingham,
> Whose figure even this instant cloud puts on
> By dark'ning my clear sun.
>
> (I, i, 223–26)

This lament is renewed in II, i as he returns from his trial, points out how quickly friends desert a man in adversity, and bids his friends

> when you would say something that is sad,
> Speak how I fell.
>
> (II, i, 135–36)

No sooner has Buckingham made his exit than the ever-present court gossips eagerly pick at the rumor of divorce between Katherine and Henry, a rumor verified in II, iii, where with unconscious irony Anne Boleyn asserts:

> By my troth and maidenhead,
> I would not be a queen.

Katherine, pressed by the two cardinals to accept divorce, bursts out against her fate, comparing herself to "the lily/ That once was mistress of the field and flourished."

Wolsey's fall is as sudden as if he were struck by lightning. He recognizes that

> I have touched the highest point of all my
>     greatness,
> And from that full meridian of my glory
> I haste now to my setting. I shall fall
> Like a bright exhalation in the evening,
> And no man see me more.
>
> (III, ii, 223–27)

A short time later, after a bitter exchange with the Duke of Norfolk and the Earl of Surrey, he comments on the insecurity of those who hang on princes' favor:

> And when he falls, he falls like Lucifer,
> Never to hope again.
>
> (III, ii, 371–72)

Such declamatory emphasis on the falls of those in high place is reenforced in a number of ways. First of all, there is the putative continuation of the series in the plot against Cranmer, which, even though he survives, gives further evidence of the transiency of power. Equally important is the mention of others whom the audience would remember as having also fallen. In his last scene, Wolsey is attended by Thomas Cromwell, who after a brief span of power was beheaded in 1540. In quick succession, Cromwell tells Wolsey of the newcomers to royal favor: Sir Thomas More (beheaded in 1535), Archbishop Cranmer (burned to death in 1556 under Queen Mary), and Anne Boleyn (beheaded in 1536). (It must be added that of Wolsey's tormenters earlier in the scene, the Earl of Surrey was beheaded in 1547 and the Duke of Norfolk escaped a like fate only because of the death of the king.)

A similarly suggestive expansion accompanies the spectacle of Anne's coronation. One of the gentlemen onlookers reminds another that the last time they met they saw the Duke of Buckingham come from his trial. Then they discuss Katherine's fate and, without emotional transition, stand gaping at the new queen as she moves by. There is a strange provocative comment as the Second Gentleman says of the queen's attendants:

> These are stars indeed.

To which the First Gentleman rejoins:

> And sometimes falling ones.

The reply is a terse and embarrassed: "No more of that."

With Anne's sorry fate only three years away, logic would seem to dictate that her fall be the fourth in the series of dramatic exempla about the falls of princes. Since it was clearly impossible to go so far, perhaps covert suggestion was left to fill in the picture. But, overt or covert, this repudiation of the idea that men are masters of their fate and can seize the tide that leads on to fortune is nothing short of astonishing in a play that celebrates the Tudor Queen Elizabeth and perhaps served as a festive adornment for the marriage of Princess Elizabeth Stuart. It is as though the shadow of the guillotine had fallen on Marie-Antoinette as she was married in Notre-Dame.

## The Life and Death of King John

The reign of King John (1199–1216) was a troubled one in four respects. He was not the direct legal heir to the throne and felt insecure on that account. For this reason and others, the French seized the opportunity to make war on him in his French territories and ultimately to invade England. There was a long-drawn-out conflict between John and the Pope, at the end of which the king had to submit to papal authority. Finally, the nobles rose against the king and extracted from him the bill of rights that we know as Magna Carta.

Descent of title for king or noble was governed by male primogeniture; that is, inheritance went from first son to first son as long as the line was unbroken, then back to second son and his male descendants, and so on. This procedure for handing on the kingship was violated only three times from 1066 to 1553. John's case was the most glaring violation. When Richard the Lionhearted died without legitimate sons in 1199, the next in line was Arthur, the twelve-year-old son of Richard's and John's deceased brother Geoffrey. Only if Arthur died without issue would John have a clear right to the throne (and to those lands and titles that Arthur had inherited in France). However, in a feudal society to put a boy king on the throne was an invitation to disaster, since a ruler's chief responsibilities were to lead in war and to keep his brawling nobles under control. Thus King Richard had designated John as his heir. Dowager Queen Elinor immediately exerted herself to win the support of the nobles in England, and John in France grabbed the royal treasure and the major English fortress towns in Normandy.

Not unnaturally, Arthur's mother, Constance, turned to the French king for help. The latter was happy to oblige, seeing an opportunity to reduce or remove English power on the Continent. Later, when he saw more advantage in a marriage between the Dauphin (the French equivalent of the Prince of Wales) and John's niece Blanch, he promptly deserted Arthur, who was fobbed off with the empty titles of Duke of Brittany and Count of Anjou, for which he did homage to John in 1200. Two years later, however, there was a renewal of the conflict; the boy was captured and imprisoned by John; and early in 1203 he died under suspicious circumstances at the English fortress at Rouen.

John's struggle with the papacy came much later. Beginning in 1205 there was a dispute between John and the Pope over who had the right to appoint the Archbishop of Canterbury. Historically, this dispute dragged on for years and did not come to a head until the summer of 1211, when Cardinal Pandulph came to England as the Pope's emissary in an effort to settle the problem. Failing to change John's position, the cardinal went to France to enlist the aid of the French. With the French arrayed against him, John had to submit in 1212, handing over his crown to Pandulph, who kept it for five days, before permitting John to resume his kingly role.

Even though England was now in the good graces of the Pope, the French were determined to carry out the invasion of England that they had been preparing with the Pope's blessing. In spite of Pandulph's opposition and threats, they persisted, landing in May 1216 and overrunning southeast England with great speed. Many English nobles went over to their side, and it looked as though the French might conquer all of England when they suffered severe setbacks and decided to withdraw. This did not occur, in fact, until September 1217, almost a year after John's death.

The restiveness of the nobility was a long-standing condition. Many were uneasy over John's seizing the throne and were all too ready to blame him for Arthur's death. Since Richard had been an absentee king during his ten-year reign, they found John's rule high-handed and oppressive. Thus they took advantage of the king's troubles with the Pope and with the French to force him to give them a charter of liberties and rights. Interestingly enough, the Pope, now on John's side, annulled the charter and excommunicated the barons who supported it—without success. What the barons had won they held in perpetuity.

The play presents all these situations and events except for the signing of Magna Carta (which looms larger to modern consciousness than it did in Shakespeare's day). But Shakespeare telescopes time in such a fashion that separate involvements seem to be a continuous action. This is achieved particularly by bringing in Pandulph at the height of the early conflict with the French while Arthur is still alive.

Only one major character is invented. He is Philip Faulconbridge—renamed Richard Plantagenet by John—who, however, is the invention of the anonymous author of the source play, *The Troublesome Reign of John, King of England*. Many of the characters, to be sure, are modified to suit the dramatic action. Arthur, for example, was not a gentle introspective boy—he was arrogant and contentious. The circumstances of Blanch's marriage are completely at variance with the facts of history (she was not even present at the meeting of the kings). Arthur's jailor Hubert was, in fact, a man of distinguished position, not the subservient creature of the play. The French king and Dauphin are stereotypes, differing only in age and degree of fire-eating intransigence. Pandulph is the stereotype of Jesuitical casuistry and intrigue. John himself—in history and in the play a puzzling character—nonetheless fits fairly well within the framework set down by Holinshed in his *Chronicle*:

> He was comely of stature, but of look and countenance displeasant and angry; somewhat cruel of nature, as by the writers of his time he is noted; and not so hardy as doubtful in time of peril and danger.

The first half of the play is straightforward and all of a piece, since it concentrates on John's resistance against the French in their support of Arthur. The opening scene in England raises this problem as a French ambassador arrogantly demands that John surrender all his territories in England, Ireland, and France to the rightful heir. John's reply is one of heartwarming defiance as he tells the ambassador

> Be thou as lightning in the eyes of France,
> For, ere thou canst report, I will be there.
> The thunder of my cannon shall be heard.
> So, hence! Be thou the trumpet of our wrath
> And sullen presage of your own decay.
> (I, i, 24–28)

An interesting change of pace occurs with the arrival of two country gentlemen, the Faulconbridge
brothers, who ask the king to settle a dispute over
their inheritance. The upshot is that the king and
Queen Elinor discern in Philip Faulconbridge unmis-
takable traits of Richard the Lionhearted. Philip hap-
pily accepts his apparent bastardy, permits his brother
to have his inheritance, and declares his support of the
king, by whom he is knighted on the spot as Sir Richard Plantagenet. In a private scene the latter forces his
mother to confirm his bastardy and congratulates her
on her infidelity since he is the result.

Action shifts to France, where the armies of England and France are encamped before the city of
Angiers. Each king demands that the townspeople declare their loyalty. They cannily refuse to do so until
they know which army has won. Faulconbridge then
suggests that the two armies band together for the
moment to subdue the refractory citizens. He is
mightily amused when the French and their Austrian
allies so dispose their forces that they will shoot at
each other from north and south. The townspeople,
thus threatened, come up with a solution that will
spare their city. They propose a marriage between the
Dauphin and Blanch, the daughter of John's sister.
John ratifies this by ceding several provinces as her
dowry, and the French, who only moments before
have been boasting of their high principles, con-
veniently forget Arthur's claims and make peace with
England.

This somewhat windy political and military conflict
is given a more human dimension by mutual recrimi-
nations between Queen Elinor and Constance, her
daughter-in-law, who bandy insults like fishwives.
Faulconbridge also expends his ingenuity in taunting
Austria, who (according to the play, though not in
fact) was the slayer of Richard the Lionhearted.

It is at this midpoint of the play that Cardinal Pandulph arrives on scene—most unhistorically—and the whole tone and emphasis of the drama changes, in a fracture so severe that directors are hard put to fuse the two parts together. Up to this point, the play is refreshing in its irreverence, astonishingly modern in the way it punctures pompous attitudes and utterance. The key figure is Faulconbridge, an unconventional commoner and a bastard, who erupts into the formality of court and battle. He does not hesitate to assert his bastardy or to renounce his inheritance when John and Elinor accept him as King Richard's son. His situation is equated with that of John, one of whose nicknames was John Lackland, when Faulconbridge says to his half-brother:

> My father gave me honor, yours gave land.
> (I, i, 164)

In other words, both he and King John are adventurers whose strong possession rather than their right must be their source of strength. In the subsequent interview with his mother, Faulconbridge congratulates her on her adultery, since

> Some sins do bear their privilege on earth . . .
> (I, i, 261)

This provides another parallel with John, who has sinned by usurping the crown, but presumably in the interest of a higher good, since Arthur is a minor.

Not only is Faulconbridge unconventional in his attitudes; he is a skeptical observer of and commenter on the world and its ways, which are rooted in deceit, as he says in his first soliloquy. He speedily gets an eyeful of deceit in the confrontation before Angiers. His immediate response is to single out strutting Austria for ridicule as a boaster and a coward. Then, fed up with the warlike utterances of both kings, he points out that they have no sense of the consequences of war when they beat their breasts in defiance:

> Ha, majesty! How high thy glory towers
> When the rich blood of kings is set on fire!
> O now doth death line his dead chaps with
> steel!
> The swords of soldiers are his teeth, his fangs;
> And now he feasts, mousing the flesh of men
> In undetermined differences of kings.
>
> (II, i, 350–55)

Finally it is he who pierces through their impotent verbosity to suggest a joint attack on Angiers, since "this peevish town" deserves punishment for its insubordinate behavior.

In his role as chorus, Faulconbridge uses language as a means of comic deflation. Having listened to a bellicose speech from besieged Angiers (II, i, 423–54), he bursts out:

> Here's a large mouth, indeed,
> That spits forth death and mountains, rocks
> and seas,
> Talks as familiarly of roaring lions
> As maids of thirteen do of puppy-dogs . . .
> 'Zounds! I was never so bethumped with
> words
> Since I first called my brother's father dad.
>
> (II, i, 457–67)

A little later he points out the artificiality of the instantaneous love match between Blanch and the Dauphin by mocking the artificial language in which the young man protests his love:

Drawn in the flattering table of her eye!
Hanged in the frowning wrinkle of her brow!
And quartered in her heart! He doth espy
Himself love's traitor; this is pity now,
That hanged and drawn and quartered, there
    should be
In such a love so vile a lout as he.

(II, i, 504–09)

His role as mocking iconoclast comes to a climax in
the soliloquy with which the scene concludes. Faulconbridge comments first on John's bad judgment in
giving up part of France in order "to stop Arthur's
title to the whole." The French are equally culpable in
that they have so readily discontinued a campaign that
they have claimed to be based on high moral principle.
But this is the way of the world. Commodity—that is,
self-interest—rules. Humorously he concludes that he
rails against it because nobody has tried to suborn him
and announces:

Since kings break faith upon commodity,
Gain, be my lord, for I will worship thee!

(II, i, 597–98)

This apparent self-revelation is ironic. Faulconbridge
is the one political leader in the play unswayed by
commodity. But he has made his point: It is a mad
world, with mad rulers, one in which honor, consis-
tency, and good sense have very little part.

King John also—up to the middle of the play—
displays a personality in reasonable harmony with this
breezy treatment of kings and warriors. He has his
share of pompous utterance, but on the whole he
comes across as a bluff, direct, and uncomplicated
being. He answers the ambassador forcefully; he suc-
cinctly analyzes the legal situation of the Faulcon-

bridge brothers; he quickly recognizes the older one's mettle and secures him to his side. He comes off less well in the general feast of windy utterance at Angiers, but his stature increases tremendously for a moment when he challenges Cardinal Pandulph and the Pope by asking

> What earthy name to interrogatories
> Can task the free breath of a sacred king?
> (III, i, 147–48)

Nothing up to this point conveys weakness. He is a warrior king like his forebears. The imperfection of his title does not greatly worry him. He has no difficulty in making up his mind. There is no evidence that he is a bad king or that his subjects are restive under his rule.

Yet with Pandulph's appearance on stage the tone of the play changes, and with it the demeanor of both John and Faulconbridge. Mockery gives way to hectic melodrama. Each scene is a set piece, a bravura performance by one or another of the characters. Blanch, newly married, suffers anguish as she is torn between loyalty to her uncle and love for the Dauphin. Constance, who has been naggingly tiresome, now soars to the outer reaches of passion, defying "all counsel, all redress" and justifying the French king's charge

> You are as fond of grief as of your child.

She tops high C in her aria of incipient madness. Then, having taken her bow, she disappears from the play. John, without the least preparation or expectation, turns into a skulking, craven, conscience-ridden prestudy of Macbeth.

There are two possible reasons for this change. One

is that the last part of the play has to cover too much. (Shakespeare is condensing a two-part play into one.) Thus continuity and motivation have to be largely abandoned in order to get everything in. More important is the emotional force generated by Pandulph. Not only is he a Machiavellian figure—an amoral intriguer—but he directly threatens John with excommunication and publicly promises that anyone who "takes away by any secret course/Thy hateful life" shall be "Canonized and worshipped as a saint." This threat, shocking in itself, leads to the treasonous desertion of some of the English nobles and to the ultimate horror of invasion by the French.

In rapid succession John is deprived of dignity and honor in four major situations. Unable to put his order to kill Arthur across to Hubert in indirect terms, he finally comes out melodramatically with the words "Murder," "A grave." Then at the emotional high point of the play comes a scene in which Arthur dissuades Hubert from putting out his eyes, a scene staged with the gruesome paraphernalia of torture. This is the first the audience has heard about blinding Arthur, a confusion that is compounded by Hubert's sudden change of heart. At the end of the episode, there is a further screwing up of pathos as the boy jumps to his death just at the point at which John is willing to guarantee his safety.

Of less intensity but equally demeaning are the scenes in which John attempts to justify his being crowned for a second time—a confession of weakness and of failure of nerve, his nobles tell him. Next there is his yielding up the crown to Pandulph, which makes an English king a mere vassal of the Pope. Finally there is his indecisive behavior during the French invasion, when he is so distraught that Faulconbridge has to urge him to act like a king.

These scenes are all necessary as part of the national legend (which includes also the belief that John was poisoned by a monk). Dramatically, as they degrade John they raise Faulconbridge to heroic heights. Faulconbridge is the only one to withhold judgment about John's guilt when he sees Arthur's battered body. He it is who takes over direction of the kingdom when John goes to pieces. And it is he who loyally sees to it that Henry III, John's minor son, ascends the throne in legal continuity after John's death.

This contrast between John and his bastard nephew, which in production must be emphasized visually as well as in terms of character, is certainly central to the last part of the play. Faulconbridge is in a position to usurp the throne when John dies. That he does not is one clear point made by the play. If we wish to read into this a lesson for the England of the 1590s, it would be: Don't rock the boat when Queen Elizabeth dies, but allow the legitimate successor to ascend the throne.

Beyond this cautionary relevance there is the question of the audience's response to and evaluation of King John himself. In the spectators' minds there was a traditional stereotype of "bad King John," not the John who was forced to concede Magna Carta—of which they had never heard—but a monarch generally bloody and tyrannical. However divergent from this the first half of the play is, the intended murder of Arthur and the desertion of the nobles support this view, which is reinforced by the vivid portrayal of John's remorse and failure of nerve. This raises serious questions about kingship. What is a good king anyway? Which is more important, his strong possession or his right? What can be done about a tyrant? These questions are never answered. Rather the audience is left with a series of images and contrasts to sort out as best it can.

For the purposes of this play Richard the Lion-hearted is a touchstone of regal excellence. John, his brother and successor, is overshadowed by him, but Faulconbridge is literally in Richard's image. We are permitted the speculation that if Richard had lived, England would not have suffered the disorder she experienced under John. And we are encouraged in the expectation that Faulconbridge, a true Plantagenet even though a bastard, will take over on John's death. This makes the affirmation of legitimate succession all the more emphatic.

There was current also another and more recent view of John as a sort of hero of the Reformation, by reason of his resistance to papal authority. There is a suggestion of conflict between king and church in the first scene when John says that the abbeys and priories shall be forced to provide money for the French campaign. The conflict springs to life with Pandulph's threat of excommunication and incitement to assassination. This hits a raw nerve of contemporary feeling, since Queen Elizabeth had been so excommunicated and threatened in 1570. John's reply to Pandulph is couched in terms that she would have used:

> But as we under heaven are supreme head,
> So under Him that great supremacy,
> Where we do reign, we will alone uphold,
> Without th'assistance of a mortal hand.
>
> (III, i, 155 ff)

Pandulph is the archetype of papist casuistry and intrigue. He manipulates rulers without scruple for truth or honor. The audience actually sees him dominating the English king, standing above him in power as he receives the crown and hands it back again to the almost prostrate John. This is a shocker to Elizabethan eyes, for it is precisely what they have feared, or have been told to fear, might happen if the Spanish fleet, blessed by the Pope, was successful.

Thus John, even though abject before Pandulph, gains a certain stature as antipapist and patriot. There is no way to reconcile the two evaluations of him that the play provides, since there is no psychological analysis that might establish how a king may be a bad man and a good patriot. The way out of this impasse is to blur inconsistency by resort to contemporary analogy. John was a weak king; his title was suspect; there was disunity at home; he had to knuckle under to the Pope when English soil was profaned by foreign armies sent by the Pope.

On the other hand, Elizabeth is a strong queen; her right to the throne is clear (though there is anxiety about the succession). There is no disunity at home, at least officially. And as legal supreme head of the English church, she has knuckled down to no one, though imperiled for a time by Catholic threats from abroad. Inescapably, this comparison underlines England's blessed state under the last of the Tudors and brings forth a flood of patriotic emotion that is given memorable expression in Faulconbridge's speech that ends the play:

> This England never did, nor never shall,
> Lie at the proud foot of a conqueror
> But when it first did help to wound itself.
> Now these her princes are come home again,
> Come the three corners of the world in arms,
> And we shall shock them. Nought shall make
>      us rue
> If England to itself do rest but true.
>
> (V, vii, 112–18)

# THE ENGLISH HISTORY
# PLAYS ON STAGE

Our notions about production in Shakespeare's day are mainly inferential, based on what we know, or think we know, about the theatrical companies and the stages that they used. Both the makeup of the companies and their stages, in fact, had an important part in the way plays were put together as well as in the way they were presented.

Shakespeare's company and its rivals were what we now call repertory groups, in which the senior members were theoretically equal and could therefore expect adequate opportunities for their particular talents as actors. There definitely was not a star system, though it is true that in Shakespeare's company the great roles of the tragedies (and of Richard III) seem to have been reserved for Richard Burbage. The necessity to cater to the requirements of fellow actors is in itself enough to account for the comic scenes in serious plays. One can hear an actor asking the dramatist about the play he is working on: "What's in it for me, Will?" and imagine his complaints if he is too long relegated to the sidelines. The greater variety of roles provided by the comic sequences in *2 Henry VI*, for example, suggests Shakespeare's attempt to meet such complaints as he worked his way into the new genre of the history play.

There was also an innate limitation by reason of the use of boys to take women's parts, a limitation that extended to the whole range of Elizabethan and Jacobean drama. No play has many female parts, presumably because no company had many apprentices capable of taking on such roles. The only stellar female role in all of Shakespeare is that of Cleopatra. In the histories, only the roles of Queen Margaret in the Henry VI plays and Queen Katherine in *Henry VIII* approach major dimensions. Shakespeare's most common practice, however, was to handle female roles so that continuing presence on stage and sustained acting were not demanded.

The physical limitations and peculiarities of the Elizabethan stage are another shaping factor. In all the histories except *Henry VIII* there is military action. Yet no stage is big enough to give a sense of the massive encounter of two armies. Thus the fighting has to be reduced to the level of individual combat in a rapid succession of personal encounters as the sword-wielding combatants run on and off stage parrying each other's blows. Repeated movement has to substitute for mass.

The amusing, if vexing, problem of how to dispose of bodies also had its effect on the plays. Since in the Elizabethan theater and its modern counterpart there was no curtain to be rung down, the bodies had to be removed by the actors on scene, as we see in the tragedies and histories alike. Hamlet lugs off Polonius after he has stabbed him through the arras. Falstaff shoulders the dead Hotspur, whom he claims as his victim. Henry IV is led off scene so that he can die in the Jerusalem chamber. After Richard II is killed, there are three bodies to dispose of. The stage direction is contained in the text as Exton orders that the two servants be carried off for burial and himself undertakes to bear "the dead king to the living king." Similarly, after killing Jack Cade, Iden tells us that he will drag Cade away and then cut off his head. Sometimes after mass carnage there is an awkward heaving up of many bodies by attendant lords and soldiers before the action can continue. For this reason, a good many killings are done off stage. A bloody severed head triumphantly brought *on* stage as evidence is easier to handle than a dead body. The theater property rooms must have been well supplied with dummy heads.

The physical conformation of the Elizabethan playhouse had its influence on the staging of a play. Not only was there no curtain, there was no scenery, and there were virtually no properties. Thus the action was continuous, without waits for scene-shifting. If necessary, change of place was indicated by the lines themselves; most frequently it did not matter or could be inferred from who was on stage. Plays that in the nineteenth- and twentieth-century era of elaborate settings needed four hours for presentation occupied much less time, could be performed uncut, and had the further advantage of rapidity of action.

The stage itself was a rectangle—an apron—wider than it was deep, jutting out into the audience. Dressing rooms may have been beneath it. Entrances and exits took place from the sides at the back. Behind the stage was a permanent three-story structure that masked behind-the-scenes activity and permitted some variety in deploying actors and creating a stage picture. On ground level was an inner chamber that could apparently be shut off by a tapestry, the pulling back of which permitted a character to be "discovered," as in the case of King Claudius at prayer in

*Hamlet* or Falstaff fast asleep after the sheriff's visit in *1 Henry IV*. This concealment made it possible to set up more elaborate and individualized scenes than were possible on the forestage. There is difference of opinion, however, as to whether actions of any great duration could go on in this recess because of the problem of voice projection.

At the second-story level was a balcony—perhaps a catwalk would be a better description—which permitted action to go on at two levels at once. It is from this elevation that the gunner's boy shoots Salisbury in *1 Henry VI*. It is there that Richard III stands between two holy bishops as he waits to be entreated to take the crown. It is from there that Richard II, after a colloquy with Aumerle, descends to the courtyard in capitulation to Bolingbroke. There was additionally a parapet at the top of the background structure that could also be used, though perhaps only for ceremonial purposes. It is at one of these upper levels that inhabitants of besieged towns shout defiance and the victors show themselves in flag-waving jubilation. It is there that heads of traitors are impaled.

The stage itself had a number of trapdoors, particularly useful for the appearance and disappearance of spirits. In *King John* when young Arthur jumps to his death, it is through one of these traps. In spite of such useful variations, most of the action took place on the stage proper, at about the eye level of spectators standing in the pit, without sets and with only the scantiest properties. We must remember too that these plays were performed in daylight (at the popular theaters), so that torches, the only kind of lighting available, had minimal effect. It was a spare and spartan setting for the vast enterprises of history, as the Chorus admits at the beginning of *Henry V*, when he entreats the audience:

Still be kind,
And eke out our performance with your mind.

Nonetheless, history plays in particular afford opportunities for spectacle. The presence of kings and nobles connotes elaborate ritual and pageantry. Kings rarely move about unattended or, on the Elizabethan stage, uncrowned. Pomp attends them with torches, banners, trumpets, heralds, and gorgeously appareled courtiers and knights at arms. Thus even on the Elizabethan stage there were many opportunities to dazzle the eye of the beholder, and, producers being what they are, there is every reason to believe that they took advantage of those opportunities, on occasion subordinating action to sheer spectacle.

Their chief resource was costume. In Shakespeare's day it was the custom for actors to wear contemporary costume, a convention that, in fact, continued until the early nineteenth century, when the romantic cult of the past encouraged the innovation of costuming for period. In the eighteenth century, for example, John Philip Kemble played Richard III in silk knee breeches, and so did David Garrick. On Shakespeare's stage, the actors were strutting peacocks, bearing their rather meager fortunes on their backs but thereby lending brilliance to the scene.

The acting, so far as we can judge, was stylized and declamatory, as is attested by the number of set speeches in many of the plays, especially the early histories. Speeches of seventy lines or more are not uncommon, and they were probably not much alleviated by business on the part of background characters. It is likely that for certain of the major roles long-continuing conventions of interpretation and costume existed. To cite one example, after the theaters reopened in 1660, continuity with Shakespeare's age was maintained by reliance on the recollection and advice of "old Mr. Lowin," that is, John Lowin, who was an interpreter of Falstaff during Shakespeare's lifetime and who lived on until 1653.

However, the eighteen-year-long closing of the theaters from 1642 to 1660, imposed by the Puritan Commonwealth, did break continuity in certain important respects. After the reopening women were permitted to take female roles. The star system became increasingly important. The theaters themselves changed their appearance and capacities with the advent of the proscenium-arch stage. Shakespeare's histories were largely out of favor, partly because of their mixture of genres, partly because of the increasing remoteness of the Wars of the Roses, and partly because they did not offer many stellar roles. It was the actor Thomas Betterton who kept Shakespeare alive after the Restoration; he played Hotspur and Falstaff among other roles. Samuel Pepys noted in his diary that he saw *Henry V* on December 28, 1666.

In 1700 a version of *Richard III* put together by Colley Cibber began a career on the boards that lasted for two centuries. During that period, when the great Shakespearean actors went in for heavy roles, among the histories *Richard III* was far and above their favorite. Virtually every actor of note essayed it—in Cibber's version. This was a concoction that drew from *3 Henry VI*, the plays of the Henriad, *Richard III*, and Cibber's own imagination. For generations playgoers quoted the line "Off with his head! So much for Buckingham" with relish as one of Shakespeare's finest touches. It is, of course, by Cibber, but apparently few people knew the difference.

The great David Garrick, whose acting dominated the theater in eighteenth-century England, first appeared in the Cibber version in London in 1741. At a later date, the great Sarah Siddons played Anne to his Richard. Thomas Kean produced this version in New York City in 1750. No doubt the oddest performance ever was one at the Broadway Theater in New York in 1849, in which Ellen Bateman, aged four, played Richard opposite the Henry Tudor of her sister Kate, aged six. This play was the first of Shakespeare's to be put on in Serbia, where Ira Aldridge, an American black actor, took the leading role in 1858. Edwin Booth did Richard at eighteen as a replacement for his father. Later on, John Wilkes Booth played Henry Tudor to his brother's Richard. Edwin Booth returned to the Shakespearean text (with cuts) in 1876, but Henry Irving, the other premier actor of the time, did not give up the Cibber text until 1896.

The prevalence of the proscenium-arch theater after 1660 permitted producers full license in the pursuit of spectacular effects. The text was often mangled and rearranged to give primacy to scenic effects—and to the actor-manager's role. Henry Irving spent three hundred thousand pounds on a lavish production of *Henry VIII*, in which he played Wolsey. In 1910, Beerbohm Tree did an even more spectacular version of *Henry VIII* ending with Anne Boleyn's coronation and presenting elaborate sets faithfully representing Cardinal Wolsey's palace, Blackfriars, and Westminster Abbey. In his production of *King John*, Tree inserted a tableau showing the signing of Magna Carta. The production to end all productions of *Henry V* was that of Richard Mansfield in New York City in 1900, appropriately at Madison Square Garden. The sets showed the London slums for the Eastcheap episodes, the harbor at Southampton for the opening of the second act, and an elaborate facsimile of the cathedral at Troyes for the marriage ceremony of Henry V and Katherine. For good measure, there was a jubilant procession in dumbshow to flesh out the Chorus's account of Henry's triumphant return to London after Agincourt. The performance ran well over four hours, with long waits while the ponderous sets were changed.

Inevitably this taste for the spectacular was translated to the screen. A very early movie (1914) starred "The Eminent Tragedian Mr. Frederick Warde in Shakespeare's Play Richard III. Five reels—5000 feet— a Feature Costing $30,000 to Produce." This landmark production used 1500 people, 200 horses, and a three-masted warship. It was acclaimed at the time as excelling anything the stage could do, though it was only an amateur precursor of Laurence Olivier's stunning film of *Richard III* (1955), in which the battle scenes, filmed in Spain, had full scope. However, Olivier continued the early tradition of playing ducks and drakes with Shakespeare's text, leaving out Queen Margaret and drawing elements from *3 Henry VI* and from the Cibber version.

It is in the last fifty years that the histories have come into their own through a fortunate combination of circumstances: the foundation of repertory theaters devoted to producing Shakespeare and the emergence of an unusual number of exceptional actors who are sensitive to the needs of such productions and willing to subordinate their talents to them.

In point of fact, the spring festivals at Stratford-on-Avon began in 1879. The first history put on there, in 1883, was *1 Henry IV*. In the next sixty years *Henry V* and *Richard II* were the histories most often presented, followed fairly closely by *Richard III* and the two parts of *Henry IV*. The latter were chosen for the opening of the new Memorial Theater in 1932. When the Stratford company made its North American tours in 1929 and 1930, it brought *1 Henry IV*, *Richard II*, and *Richard III*, the first two of which had never been seen by most of the spectators. Not unreasonably, this company, now called the Royal Shakespeare Theater, chose *Henry V* for performance in the United States during the bicentennial celebrations.

For the 1951 Festival of Britain the Stratford company put on the plays of the second tetralogy—*Richard II*, *1 Henry IV*, *2 Henry IV*, and *Henry V*—in sequence, the first time this had been done since 1905. It was a remarkable gathering together of talent: Anthony Quayle as Falstaff, Richard Burton as Prince Hal/Henry V, and Michael Redgrave as Richard II and the Chorus in *Henry V*. The Old Vic, the Memorial Theater's London competitor, did all of Shakespeare's plays between 1914 and 1923, and with the omission of *Pericles* ran through them again in 1953 through 1958. In *Henry VIII* John Gielgud played Wolsey and Edith Evans Queen Katherine.

There were other notable performances in the years after 1930. At the Old Vic in 1931, Gielgud and Ralph Richardson took the parts of Hotspur and Prince Hal. During the next season Richardson played Faulconbridge in *King John* and the king in *Henry V*. In 1937, Maurice Evans electrified American audiences with his *Richard II*, last seen in New York with Edwin Booth in 1878. It ran for 171 performances and was then taken on tour. In an English production, also in 1937, Gielgud was Richard II, supported by Michael Redgrave and Peggy Ashcroft. In 1945, in the two parts of *Henry IV*, Ralph Richardson was Falstaff and Laurence Olivier was Hotspur and Justice Shallow. Alec Guinness essayed Richard II in 1946 and opened the Festival Theater at Stratford, Ontario, in 1953 in Tyrone Guthrie's production of *Richard III*. And not to be forgotten is the artistic triumph of Olivier's film *Henry V* in 1944 or the éclat of his film *Richard III* in 1955, in which he was supported by

Gielgud as Clarence, Richardson as Buckingham, Alec Clunes as Hastings, and Cedric Hardwicke as Edward IV. These are only a few of the memorable productions of that thirty-year span. The actors named reached the summit of their profession during that period, and their fame rests in significant degree on their achievements in the once-neglected history plays.

Not only did the Stratford-on-Avon theater and the Old Vic (as well as the New Old Vic) in London make it a practice to present the complete canon of Shakespeare's plays, but other companies came into being with the same goals. The Birmingham Repertory Company in England, the Festival Theater at Stratford, Ontario, the American Festival Theater at Stratford, Connecticut (which came to an end in 1976), and the Oregon Festival Theater at Ashland, Oregon, have all, for periods ranging over two to four decades, put on Shakespearean seasons. The result is that almost anyone who has wanted to in England has been able to see all the histories, and that North Americans, east and west, have, with a little more effort and expense, had the same opportunity.

This availability is particularly to be noted in respect to minor plays such as the three parts of *Henry VI*, whose previous stage history may be likened to the short and simple annals of the poor. However, for the general public these plays are likely to be fused in some way with the preceding *Richard II* and *Henry IV* and the following *Richard III*. During the 1960s there was a very successful television program in England entitled *An Age of Kings* that spanned the period from Richard II to Richard III. At Stratford-on-Avon in 1963, John Barton made an arrangement of the *Henry VI* plays and *Richard III* called *The Wars of the Roses* in three parts. This production was a great triumph and gave the character of Queen Margaret, as played by Peggy Ashcroft, a coherence that it does not have when the plays are presented in isolation.

Although modern productions have been much more faithful to the texts and to Elizabethan conventions of staging than their predecessors, they have not escaped gimmickry. A production of *Henry V* at the First Mermaid Theater in London in 1960 succumbed to the vogue for modern dress. Hal greeted the Archbishop of Canterbury in cricket flannels; the battle dress was updated; and the Chorus attempted a rendition of "Roses of Picardy" on the mouth-organ. A recent production of *King John* invested John's death with the solemnity of a chanting procession of monks —singularly inappropriate considering the reputed cause of his death.

The unprecedented availability of the histories on stage is not proof absolute of renewed interest on the part of audiences. Shakespeare has become big business at the Stratfords and at Ashland. Though it can be noticed that the attention of spectators frequently wanders and that entr'acte conversations sometimes express more bewilderment than understanding, still the audiences keep coming—even to *Henry VI*. It is likely that beneath the pomp and the recondite events of these plays audiences do discern relevance to the twentieth century. Our power struggles are not dynastic, and they are on a scale inconceivable to the adherents of York and Lancaster. Still if we are sometimes confused by the details of those ancient conflicts, they do show the age-old maneuvers of men who have power, who lose it, or who try to gain it. Just as *Coriolanus* has become popular in our time, because it deals with problems of dictatorship, so the English histories have an interest for twentieth-century audiences.

It is possible to argue that in addition to the predilections of actors and producers of an earlier day, eighteenth-century belief in rationality and nineteenth-century bourgeois decorum blunted the impact of these plays, and that the incipient social chaos and the unblushing exercise of naked power of our own times have resensitized us to them. Even more important is the matter of scale. Social disaster in our day is so vast as to be incommensurable; it dwarfs victims and victimizers alike. It is mechanical, nonhuman, unintelligible.

But the social disasters Shakespeare portrays are on a smaller scale. Men are the agents of their own destruction or redemption. Their motives are recognizable. Their power has manifest limits. Above all they inhabit a moral universe. Though intellectually we may scoff at such a providential view of history as simple, even shallow, emotionally we respond to it and find comfort in it.

# PERSPECTIVES

The first nine English history plays constitute one-half of Shakespeare's production during his first decade as dramatist. They provided him an opportunity for experiment not readily available in his concurrent efforts at comedy and tragedy, where he was bound by the rules. The appeal of attested historical fact helped to obscure and outweigh lack of finesse in the handling of language, dramatic organization, and characterization.

It is a far cry from the mechanical, mannered, and declamatory verse of the three parts of *Henry VI* to the terse, flexible, human utterance of *1* and *2 Henry IV*. There is a steady movement away from the static, if passionate, figures of the early histories to many-faceted characters such as Hotspur, Falstaff, and Richard II. There is no question that Shakespeare learned his craft by practicing it and that a large part of his learning came from dealing with the recalcitrant materials of history.

In spite of the Elizabethan fondness for labeling plays as "true tragedies" or "true chronicle histories," such an attribution of character is essentially anti-dramatic. As Dr. Johnson has pointed out:

> History was a series of actions, with no other than chronological succession, independent on each other, and without any tendency to introduce or regulate the conclusion. It is not always very nicely distinguished from tragedy. There is not much nearer approach to unity of action in the tragedy of *Antony and Cleopatra*, than in the history of *Richard the Second*. But a history might be continued through many plays; as it had no plan, it had no limits.

In other words, chronicle history has only a linear pattern, a linear logic. Event B comes after event A in a series that runs on to infinity, though the death of a king for Shakespeare and his contemporaries provides a convenient stopping place.

Thus it is that Shakespeare's ten histories are, indeed, organized, however casually, around the reigns of various monarchs. Whatever the dramatist ultimately learned about handling linear events, he was in the first instance confined by the events of a reign. In all cases, when the king dies, the play stops. Whereas *Lear* and *Macbeth*, though based on nebulous chronicle materials, are regulated as to the conclusion, that is, shaped to produce the catharsis of tragedy, *Richard III* and *King John* are not so regulated. At the end of these two plays, the emphasis is not on the death of a great man but on what that death means to the kingdom. As one critic has pertinently observed, in the history plays we are dealing with values that have to do with politics, not personal ethics.

In any event, to label a play a "true tragedy" or "true history" is to obscure the main issue. George Bernard Shaw once wrote Upton Sinclair—who was addicted to the true-fact, reportorial method—that records of fact are not history. They are only annals, which have no artistic or philosophical validity until they are rescued "from the unintelligible chaos of their actual occurrence" and arranged into the forms of art. It is such a rescue from unintelligible chaos that is proof of Shakespeare's developing dramatic skill.

The tendency of early writers of chronicle plays to crowd in as many episodes as possible is present in the three *Henry VI* plays. If not unintelligible, they are confused and lack dramatic focus. To a lesser degree this is true of *King John*, written about the same time.

From that point on, in Shakespeare's use of historical material there is steady movement away from the chronicle format toward a use of historical materials as a platform for a coherent and limited dramatic action. He learns to leave out events; he learns to invent illustrative episodes; he telescopes the actual time scheme in such a way that events scattered over a period of years seem to be a continuous action. Not only does he provide a chronological framework for the two tetralogies; for the second (the one beginning with *Richard II*) he provides a philosophical framework as well. He goes further than any of his contemporaries in exploring the possibilities of the genre. His mastery of it is equal to his mastery of romantic comedy and tragedy, and perhaps more impressive since he had to start from scratch. Sometimes he failed, by lack of skill or by inattention, as in *King John*. At his best he could make an essentially minor action, like the Northumberland conspiracy in *1 Henry IV*, yield observations or questions about political governance of universal significance.

Yet there appears to be a built-in limit on the moral profundity of the history play. Ultimately the subject of the falls of princes, or would-be princes, becomes banal because the political spectacle is more or less predictable. There is something repetitious about the outward show of usurpations, murders and summary executions, play-acting for advantage, and sudden reverses of worldly fortune. All these things may belong to the framework that surrounds the human condition, but they are not the human experience itself.

In proportion as Shakespeare's public figures are well realized as characters on the stage, we become impatient over their lack of rich and convincing inner life. This is exemplified in *Henry VIII*. Both Queen Katherine and Cardinal Wolsey are brilliantly brought to life—up to a point. But it is beyond that point that we want to know them. The tears of things are in the private anguish, not the public spectacle; in the unique individual, not the generic example. What is it like, having been wife and queen in a foreign land for more than twenty years, suddenly to be repudiated, to be shipwrecked on an alien shore? What is it like for a man who has pulled himself up from an Ipswich butcher shop to the very pinnacles of priestly and worldly power suddenly to plummet back to the indifferent earth? Or for that matter, what is it like in the case of Henry V to bestride two realms like a colossus and perhaps, like Alexander, to sigh for new worlds to conquer?

By and large there is no empathetic union with the major figures in the history plays because we know them insufficiently as private men and women. Shakespeare spares little time for more than casual humanizing touches as he moves them through their appointed public roles. Even their soliloquies are public utterances, reviews of policy or studied commentary on the responsibilities that hedge a king. Only occasionally is the formality of state broken by a revealing cry of anguish: Wolsey's final words to Cromwell; Henry

V's "Upon the king!" speech before he settles into reasoned analysis; Falstaff's being shocked into honest admission: "Master Shallow, I owe you a thousand pound"; Richard II for a moment escaping histrionism as he visualizes Bolingbroke riding roan Barbary.

The infrequency of such passionate outbursts may be accounted for by the absence of anyone to whom these public figures may unburden themselves. Nowhere in the history plays is there an intimate friend like Hamlet's Horatio. For the most part, husbands and wives are constrained to formality, the chief exception being Hotspur and Lady Percy. The one father-son relationship of importance is that of Henry IV and Prince Hal, in which there is more animosity than warmth. The instances of courtship that the plays afford reveal little about the emotions of the kings involved. We get little more insight from seeing Hal in love than we do from seeing Falstaff in love. In general, families function only in a formal sense, and what we see is an adversary relationship, as is egregiously the case with Richard III.

In the mature tragedies, which follow in steady sequence immediately after the histories, the emphasis is reversed. While the protagonists are all public men (with the exception of Timon of Athens), their passion is private. They reveal themselves and they discover themselves as individuals, suffering the thousand natural shocks the flesh is heir to. No doubt, by the conventions of the older literature, they more readily command attention because of their high place, but ultimately high place is incidental to the intensity of their struggle. The tragic loss is double, both public and private: of Hamlet and Coriolanus as potentially great rulers; of Othello and Antony and Macbeth as leaders of men whose rough and ready grasp of certainties, needed in an uncertain world, relaxes as those certainties lose their visible shape under the impulsion of devastating private passion. Yet in all these cases the persistent image of loss is not that of the king or soldier but of a simple suffering man, purified and ennobled by what he has gone through, therefore triumphant even as he is destroyed.

The data of history resist shaping to such a vision, or at least they must be dissolved in legend, with their outlines becoming fluid enough to permit reshaping. When Shakespeare deserted Holinshed for Plutarch, he somehow found the latter's facts less recalcitrant, partly because they were less immediate in time, partly because Plutarch had already wrested them into a moral pattern. Certainly, the data of Shakespeare's sources for *Hamlet*, *Othello*, *Lear*, and *Macbeth* were unresistant, allowing a latitude of treatment not possible in the history plays.

Shakespeare could examine one moral impasse after another, fleshing out the dramatic action with parallels of family life in *Hamlet* and *Lear*, involving the supernatural in *Macbeth*, equating sordid domestic disorder with philosophical chaos in *Othello*. He could invent scenes and characters to give his protagonists multiple dimensions, and he could leave out anything that was not immediately relevant to the understanding of human experience to which the play led. Equally important, he had learned to use language that was flexible and varied, individual in tone, responsive to private emotion, not declamatory for public effect. There are passages in the histories in which the language reaches the level just described, but they are infrequent, just as revelation of the inner being is infrequent.

This is not to demean the histories by seeing them merely as an exploratory treatment of serious subjects in preparation for the ultimate seriousness of the tragedies. They have their own strengths and their own vision. They do illuminate the past, in a general as well as in a specific way. They can be exciting experiences in the theater when they are performed according to the logic they contain, not subject to overwhelming weight of spectacle, to facile modernizing, or to distortion in the interest of a single stellar role.

# BIBLIOGRAPHY

*All scene and line references are to* The Pelican Shake-speare, *Penguin Books Inc.*

*1. First printings of Shakespeare's histories*

*1 Henry VI:* appeared in print only in the First Folio, 1623.

*2 Henry VI:* THE First part of the Contention betwixt the two famous Houses of Yorke and Lancaster, with the death of the good Duke Humphrey: And the banishment and death of the Duke of *Suffolke*, and the Tragicall end of the proud Cardinall of *VVinchester*, vvith the notable Rebellion of Iacke *Cade: And the Duke of Yorkes first claime vnto the Crowne*, 1594, reprinted in 1600. This is a "bad quarto," that is, a corrupt and unauthorized text.

*3 Henry VI:* The true Tragedie of Richard *Duke of Yorke*, and the death of good King Henrie the Sixt, *with the whole contention betweene* the two Houses of Lancaster and Yorke, as it was sundrie times acted by the Right Honourable the Earle of Pembrooke his seruants, 1595, reprinted in 1600. Another "bad quarto." In 1619 the two plays were issued together as The Whole Contention be-tweene the two Famous Houses, Lancaster and Yorke.

*Richard III:* THE TRAGEDY OF King Richard the

third. Containing, His treacherous Plots against his brother Clarence: the pittiefull murther of his innocent nephewes: his tyrannicall vsurpation: with the whole course of his detested life, and most deserued death. As it hath beene lately Acted by the Right honourable the Lord Chamberlaine his seruants, 1597. Reissued in 1598 (with "William Shake-speare" on the title page), 1602, 1605, 1612, 1622.

*King John:* appeared in print only in the First Folio, 1623.

*Richard II:* THE Tragedie of King Richard the second. *As it hath beene publikely acted by the right Honourable the Lorde Chamberlaine his Seruants.* 1597. Reissued twice in 1598, with "By William Shakespeare" on the title page. The fourth quarto in 1608 adds the following: "With new additions of the Parliament Sceane, and the deposing of King Richard, As it hath been lately acted by the Kinges Majesties seruantes, at the Globe." There was a fifth quarto in 1615.

*1 Henry IV:* THE HISTORY OF HENRIE THE FOVRTH; With the battell at Shrewsburie, *betweene the King and Lord* Henry Percy, surnamed Henrie Hotspur of the North. *With the humorous conceits* of Sir John Falstalffe, 1598. There were two editions in 1598 and five more before the First Folio.

*2 Henry IV:* THE Second part of Henrie the fourth, continuing to his death, *and coronation of Henrie* the fift. With the humours of sir Iohn *Falstaffe, and swaggering Pistoll. As it hath been sundrie times publikely* acted by the right honourable, the Lord Chamberlaine his seruants. *Written by William Shakespeare,* 1600.

*Henry V:* THE CRONICLE History of Henry the fift With his battell fought at *AginCourt* in *France.* Togither with *Auntient Pistoll As it hath bene sundry times played by the Right honorable*

*the Lord Chamberlaine his seruants,* 1600. A very corrupt quarto, reissued in 1602 and 1619.
*Henry VIII:* appeared in print only in the First Folio, 1623.

Heminge, John, and Condell, Henry (eds.), Mr. William SHAKESPEARES COMEDIES, HISTORIES, & TRAGEDIES. Published according to the True Originall Copies. 1623. This is the famous First Folio.

## 2. Works about Shakespeare*

Alexander, Peter, *Shakespeare's Henry VI and Richard III*, Cambridge: Cambridge University Press, 1929.
Altick, R. D., "Symphonic Imagery in *Richard II*," *PMLA* 62 (1947): 339–65.
Armstrong, W. A. (ed.), *Shakespeare's Histories: An Anthology of Modern Criticism*, Harmondsworth: Penguin Shakespeare Library, 1972.
Barber, C. L., *Shakespeare's Festive Comedy*, "Rule and Misrule in *Henry IV*," pp. 192–221, Cleveland: World Publishing Company, 1963.
Bevington, David, *Tudor Drama and Politics: A Critical Approach to Topical Meaning*, Cambridge: Harvard University Press, 1968.
Bonjour, Adrien, "The Road to Swinstead Abbey; a Study of the Sense and Structure of *King John*," *ELH* 18 (1951): 253–74.
Boswell-Stone, W. G., *Shakespeare's Holinshed: The Chronicle and the Historical Plays Compared*, New York: Benjamin Blom, Inc., 1966 (first published in 1896).
Bradley, A. C., *Oxford Lectures on Poetry*, "The Re-

---

* With very few exceptions the bibliography is drawn from scholarship of the last thirty years.

jection of Falstaff," pp. 247–53, London: Macmillan, 1909; second edition, 1950.

Bromley, John C., *The Shakespearean Kings*, Boulder, Colo.: Colorado Associated Universities Press, 1971.

Campbell, Lily B., *Shakespeare's "Histories": Mirrors of Elizabethan Policy*, San Marino, Cal.: The Huntington Library, 1947.

Clemen, Wolfgang (Bonheim, Jean, translator), *A Commentary on Shakespeare's Richard III*, London: Methuen, 1968.

———, *English Tragedy before Shakespeare*, London: Methuen, 1961.

Dorius, R. J. (ed.), *Discussions of Shakespeare's Histories: Richard II to Henry V*, Boston: Heath 1964.

———, "Prudence and Excess in *Richard II* and the Histories," *Sh. Q.* 11 (Winter 1960): 13–26.

Driver, Tom F., *The Sense of History in Greek and Shakespearean Drama*, New York: Columbia University Press, 1960.

Grebanier, Bernard, *Then Came Each Actor*, New York: David McKay, 1975.

Gurr, Andrew, *The Elizabethan Stage 1574–1642*, Cambridge: Cambridge University Press, 1970.

Hosley, Richard (ed.), *Shakespeare's Holinshed*, New York: Putnam, 1968.

Humphreys, A. R., *Shakespeare's "Richard II,"* London: Edward Arnold, 1967.

Hunter, G. K., "*Henry IV* and the Elizabethan Two-Part Play," *RES* n. s. 5 (1954): 236–48.

Jenkins, Harold, *The Structural Problem in Shakespeare's "Henry the Fourth,"* London: Methuen, 1956.

Jorgensen, P. A., *Shakespeare's Military World*, Berkeley: University of California Press, 1956.

Joseph, B. L., *Shakespeare's Eden: The Commonwealth of England 1558–1629*, London: Blandford Press, 1971.

Kelly, H. A., *Divine Providence in the England of Shakespeare's Histories*, Cambridge: Harvard University Press, 1970.

Knight, G. Wilson, *The Crown of Life: Interpretations of Shakespeare's Final Plays*, London: Oxford University Press, 1947.

Knights, L. C., *William Shakespeare; the Histories, Richard III, King John, Richard II, Henry V*, London: Longmans Green, 1962.

Leech, Clifford, *William Shakespeare; the Chronicles, Henry VI, Henry IV, The Merry Wives of Windsor, Henry VIII*, London: Longmans Green, 1962.

Manheim, Michael, *The Weak King Dilemma in the Shakespeare History Play*, Syracuse: Syracuse University Press, 1973.

Manvell, Roger, *Shakespeare and the Film*, New York: Praeger, 1971.

Morgann, Maurice, *Essay on the Dramatic Character of Sir John Falstaff* (1777), Fineman, D. A. (ed.), Oxford: Clarendon Press, 1972.

Ornstein, Robert, *A Kingdom for a Stage; the Achievement of Shakespeare's History Plays*, Cambridge: Harvard University Press, 1972.

Palmer, John, *Political Characters of Shakespeare*, London: Macmillan, 1945.

Pierce, R. B., *Shakespeare's History Plays: The Family and the State*, Columbus: Ohio State University Press, 1971.

Prior, Moody E., *The Drama of Power; Studies in Shakespeare's History Plays*, Evanston: Northwestern University Press, 1973.

Reese, M. M., *The Cease of Majesty: A Study of Shakespeare's History Plays*, London: Edward Arnold, 1961.

———, *The Tudors and Stuarts*, London: Edward Arnold, 1959.

Ribner, Irving, *The English History Play in the Age of Shakespeare*, revised edition, London: Methuen, 1965.

Richmond, H. M., *Shakespeare's Political Plays*, New York: Random House, 1967.

Riggs, David, *Shakespeare's Heroical Histories "Henry VI" and its Literary Tradition*, Cambridge: Harvard University Press, 1971.

Saccio, Peter, *Shakespeare's English Kings*, N.Y.: Oxford University Press, 1977.

Sen Gupta, S. C., *Shakespeare's Historical Plays*, London: Oxford University Press, 1964.

Sprague, A. C., *Shakespeare's Histories; Plays for the Stage*, London: Society for Theatre Research, 1964.

Stoll, E. E., *Shakespeare Studies: Historical and Comparative in Method*, "Falstaff," pp. 403–90, New York: Macmillan, 1927.

Talbert, E. W., *Elizabethan Drama and Shakespeare's Early Plays*, Chapel Hill: University of North Carolina Press, 1963.

Tillyard, E. M. W., *Shakespeare's History Plays*, London: Chatto & Windus, 1944.

Toliver, H. E., "Falstaff, the Prince, and the History Play," *Sh. Q.* 16 (1965): 63–80.

Traversi, Derek, *Shakespeare from Richard II to Henry V*, Stanford: Stanford University Press, 1957.

Trewin, J. C., *Shakespeare on the English Stage 1900–1964*, London: Barrie and Rockliff, 1964.

Waith, Eugene M. (ed.), *Shakespeare, The Histories: A Collection of Critical Essays*, Englewood Cliffs, N.J.: Prentice-Hall, 1965.

Wilson, John Dover, *The Fortunes of Falstaff*, New York: Macmillan, 1944.

Wilson, John Dover, and Worsley, T. C., *Shakespeare's Histories at Stratford 1951*, London: M. Reinhardt, 1952.

Winny, James, *The Player King: A Study of Shakespeare's Later History Plays*, London: Chatto & Windus, 1968.

# INDEX

acting, Shakespeare, 163–
64
Adam, Shakespeare plays, 5
*Age of Kings, An* (TV pro-
gram), 168
Agincourt (France), 66, 67,
71, 72–73, 75, 166
Alridge, Ira, 165
allusions, contemporary, 13
American Festival Theater,
168
analogy, contemporary, 158
Angiers (France), 150, 152,
154
Anne, Queen (a Stuart),
132n
Anne of Warwick (later
Lady Anne; Queen
to Richard III), 47,
106, 165
the character, 118, 122–29
illustration of, 47
Antony, 175–76
Archbishop of Canterbury.
*See:* Canterbury,
Archbishop of;
Cranmer, Thomas
Archbishop of York. *See*
York, Archbishop of
Arthur (King John's

nephew), 13, 146–49
the character, 149–58, 162
Arthur, Prince, 136
Arundel, Earl of, 16
Ashcroft, Peggy, 167, 169
Asherson, Renée, 43
Ashland, Oregon, 168, 169
*As You Like It,* 5
Aumerle. *See* Edward Duke
of Aumerle

Bardolph, 31–32, 42, 50, 73,
75, 77
Barton, John, 168–69
Bates (a soldier), 73
Beaufort, Edmund (Duke
of Somerset, d.
1455), 95–96, 103–104
the character, 96–103
Beaufort, Edmund (Duke
of Somerset, d.
1471), 107
the character, 114
Beaufort, Henry (Bishop
of Winchester; later
Cardinal), 83–84,
95–96
the character, 85–86, 96–
103
Beaufort, John (Duke of

Beaufort, John *(Cont'd)*
    Somerset), 83, 86, 87
Beaufort, Thomas (Duke of
    Exeter), 83–84
Bedford, Duke of. *See* John
    of Lancaster
Bellamy, Diana, 41
Betterton, Thomas, 164
biographical data, 3, 4, 5–6,
    8, 132
  fictional, 3–4
  speculative, 5, 12, 29
Birmingham Repertory
    Company, 168
Bishop of Winchester. *See*
    Beaufort, Henry
Blanch (King John's niece),
    147, 149
  the character, 150, 152,
    154
Bloom, Claire, 47
Blunt, Sir Walter, 38
Boleyn, Anne, 133
  the character, 136–45, 165
Bolingbroke, Henry. *See*
    Henry IV
*Book of the Hours*, 43
Booth, Edwin, 165, 167
Booth, John Wilkes, 165
Bradley, A. C., 38–39
Braek, Philip, 42
Broadway Theater, 165
Buckingham, Duke of. *See:*
    Stafford, Edward;
    Stafford, Henry;
    Stafford, Humphrey
Burbage, Richard, 2, 159
Burgess, Anthony, 3
Burton, Richard, 167

Cade, Jack, 94
  the character, 100–102,
    161
Cade Rebellion, 94, 100–102
Calais (France), 10, 67
Canterbury, Archbishop of,
    69, 70–71, 76, 79, 169.
    *See also* Cranmer,
    Thomas
characterizations, 159–60,
    174–75
  of the rabble, 101
  stereotypes in, 74–75
  in the tragedies, 175–76
Charles V (of Spain), 136
Charles VI, 82, 103, 104
Charles VII (formerly the
    Dauphin), 45, 66–68,
    82, 92
  the character, 69–70, 90–
    91
  illustration of, 45
Charles Duke of Orléans, 67
Chorus, the, 73, 79, 129,
    152, 162–63, 166, 167,
    169
*Chronicle* (Holinshed), 11,
    149. *See also* Holin-
    shed
chronicle plays. *See* histo-
    ries, the
Chugg, Gail, 45
Church, Tony, 46
Church of England, 10, 136
Cibber, Colley, 164–65, 166
Cibber text versions, 166
civil war. *See* Wars of the
    Roses
Clarence, Duke of. *See:*
    George Duke of Clar-

ence; Lionel Duke of Clarence; Thomas Duke of Clarence
Claudius (King), 161–62
Cleopatra, 160
Clifford, Lord, 103
Clifford, the young, 106
  the character, 109–111
Clunes, Alec, 168
comedies, the, 8
*Comedy of Errors, A*, 8
Condell, Henry, 2
*Coriolanus*, 169
Coriolanus, 175
costume, Shakespearean, 163
Cranmer, Thomas (Archbishop of Canterbury), 133, 136
  the character, 141–45
criticism, from contemoraries, 5
Cromwell, Thomas, 14, 144, 174

Dance, Charles, 42
Dauphin, the (13th century) 147, 149, 150, 152, 54
Dauphin, the (15th century). *See* Charles VII
Davy, 42
*deus ex machine*, the, 128, 142
Doll Tearsheet, 57–59, 62–63
  illustration of, 41
Donaldson, Tom, 40
Dorset, Marquess of, 118, 125

Douglas, Earl of, 30–31
dramaturgy, the, 49, 116, 120, 171, 176
  compression of time in, 105, 117, 173
  the *deux ex machina*, in, 128, 142
  and format, 128, 173
  functions of scenes in, 102
  and historical omissions, 103–104
  scenic aspects in, 132, 133, 141, 163
  set speeches in, 163
  stage requirements of, 160–61

Eastcheap sequences, 31–32, 35–39, 48, 49–50, 58, 75–76, 165. *See also* Gloucestershire sequences
Edmund Earl of Rutland, 106, 107
  the character, 107, 109–110
Edmund of Langley (Duke of York), 16, 84, 85
  the character, 17
Edward, Prince of Wales, 103, 106–107
  the character, 114–15
*Edward II* (Marlowe), 9
Edward III, 15–16, 21, 30n, 52, 76, 84, 85, 95, 133
Edward IV, 83, 84, 106–108, 117–19, 168
  the character, 109–115, 121–25

Edward V, 124–25
Edward Duke of Aumerle
    (later Duke of York),
    19, 22, 67
Edwards, Richard Allen, 40
Edward the Black Prince,
    15, 21
Eleanor Duchess of Glou-
    cester, 94
Elinor of Aquitaine (Queen
    to Henry II), 82, 147
  the character, 150–56
Elizabeth, Princess (a
    Stuart), 132–33, 145
Elizabeth I, Queen of En-
    gland, 11, 12, 13, 29,
    132–34, 142, 145,
    158
Elizabethan drama, 160
Elizabethan literature, 11
  function of, 9
Elizabethan stage, 160–62
Elizabeth Woodville
    (Lady Grey; later
    Queen to Edward
    IV), 106–107, 118–
    19
  the character, 124–31
Elizabeth of York (Queen
    to Henry VII), 11,
    125–26
England
  national identity of, 10
  history of. See history
Essex, Earl of, 13, 29
Evans, Edith, 167
Evans, Maurice, 167
Everyman in His Humour
    (Jonson), 2, 5
Exton, Piers, 17, 161

fall of the mighty, as theme,
    142–45, 173–74
Falstaff. See John Falstaff
Famous Victories of Henry
    V, The, 8, 32
Faulconbridge. See Philip
    Faulconbridge
Festival Theater, 167, 168
First Folio, the, 2, 3, 7
First Mermaid Theater, 169
First Part of Kiny Henry
    the Fourth, The. See
    Henry IV, Part One
Fletcher, John, 6
Fluellen (Captain), 44, 74,
    76–78
folio, 6n, 7
formality versus force, as
    theme, 19
France
  and England, 15, 66–68,
    81–82, 90, 146–49,
    150–56
  power of, 10

Gardiner, Stephen (Bishop
    of Winchester), 142
Garrick, David, 163, 164–65
Geoffrey, 146
Geoffrey of Anjou, 82
George I, 132n
George Duke of Clarence,
    106–108, 117–19, 168
  the character, 114–16,
    121–23
Ghost, the, in Shakespeare
    plays, 5
Gielgud, John, 167, 168
Glendower, Owen, 30–31
  the character, 34, 48

Globe Theater, 2, 29, 132
Gloucester, Duke of. *See:*
    Humphrey Duke of
    Gloucester; Richard
    III; Thomas of
    Woodstock
Gloucestershire sequences,
    57–60, 63
Greene, Robert, 1, 5
Grey, Lady. *See* Elizabeth
    Woodville
Grey, Lord, 118
    the character, 124, 128–30
*Groatsworth of Wit*
    (Greene), 1
Guiness, Alec, 167
Guthrie, Tyrone, 167


Hal, Prince of Wales. *See*
    Henry V
Hall, Edward, 11
*Hamlet*, 5, 162, 176
Hamlet, 13, 56, 160, 175
Hardwicke, Cedric, 168
Harfleur (France), 66, 71
Hastings, Lord (Lord
    Chamberlain), 108,
    119, 121, 168
Hathaway, Anne, 1, 4–5
Heminge, John, 2
"Henriad," the, 15n, 164
Henry III, 156
*Henry IV*, Part One, 2, 8,
    15n, 30–50, 64, 162,
    171, 173
    illustration of, 40
    productions of, 166–67,
    168

*Henry IV*, Part Two, 2, 8,
    15n, 32, 49, 51–65,
    166–67, 168, 17
    illustration of, 41, 42
Henry IV (Henry Boling-
    broke), 16, 17, 30–31,
    31n, 51, 83–84
    the character, 16–29, 33,
    48–50, 51–55, 61–62,
    160, 162, 175
*Henry V*, 8, 10, 15n, 32,
    66–80, 162–63
    film version of, 43, 79,
    80, 167
    illustrations of, 43, 4 4
    productions of, 80, 164,
    165–66, 166–67, 168
Henry V (formerly Prince
    Hal), 14, 15n, 31, 40,
    42, 43, 51, 66, 81–84,
    167
    the character, 28–29, 32–
    39, 48–50, 52–65, 68–
    80, 165, 169, 174–75
    illustrations of, 40, 42, 43
*Henry VI*, Part One, 15n,
    81–93, 95, 113, 116,
    117, 160, 162, 171, 173
    illustration of, 45
    productions of, 168, 169
*Henry VI*, Part Two, 8,
    15n, 94–104, 105, 113,
    116, 117, 159–60, 171,
    173
    productions of, 168, 169
*Henry VI*, Part Three, 8,
    15n, 105–116, 117,
    126, 160, 164, 166,
    169, 171, 173
    productions of, 168

Henry VI, 81–85, 94–96, 103–104, 105–108, 117, 118
  the character, 48, 86–92, 97–103, 108–116, 126
Henry VII (formerly Earl of Richmond), 11, 104, 116, 117–19, 165
  the character, 12, 125–28
*Henry VIII*, 6, 12, 132–45, 160, 174
  film version of, 141
  productions of, 2, 132, 165, 167
Henry VIII, 11, 12, 133–34
  the character, 135–45
histoire moralisée, 131
histories, the, 8
  authorship of, 7
  characterization in, 174–75
  contemporary reception of, 13–14, 29
  as means to mirror present, 12–13
  morality of, 10–11
  nature of, 9, 10, 12, 163, 169–70, 171–72, 176–77
  organization of, 172
  precedents for, 8–9
  relevance of, to 20th centur, 169–70
  sources for, 11–12
  and the tragedies, 171–77
history, English, 9, 10, 15–17, 30–31, 30n–31n, 51, 87, 103–104, 117–20, 132n, 132–34, 136, 157–58

with France, 15, 66–68, 81–82, 90, 146–49, 150–56
  and the Lancastrian-York-ist conflict, 83–85, 94–96, 105–108, 128
  purposes of, 11
  use of, as comment, 12–13
Holinshed, Raphael, 11, 30n, 67, 86, 107, 176
  on the Archbishop of York, 52
  on Charles VII, 92
  on Henry V, 56–57, 68–69
  on Joan of Arc, 90–91, 92
  on King John, 149
  on Richard II, 18
  on Richard III, 119–20
Horatio, 175
Hotspur. *See* Percy, Henry
Howard, Alan, 42
Humphrey Duke of Gloucester (Lord Protector), 42, 83–84, 94–96
  the character, 85–86, 96–99, 113
  illustration of, 42

Iago, 122
imagery, 25–28, 60–64
  unity of, 28–29
Irving, Henry, 165

Jacobean drama, 160
James I, 2, 132
Jenn, Stephen, 42
Joan of Arc (also La Pu-

celle), 45, 82, 87, 92
    the character, 87–92
    illustration of, 45
John, King of England,
        146–49, 156
    the character, 149–58,
        169
John Falstaff (*Henry VI*,
        Part One), 89
John Falstaff (Sir), 41, 42,
        75, 78, 160, 162, 164,
        167, 171, 175
    in *Henry IV*, Part One,
        31–39, 48–50
    in *Henry IV*, Part Two,
        51–53, 55–65
    illustrations of, 41, 42
John of Gaunt (Duke of
        Lancaster), 16, 83,
        84, 118
    the character, 17, 19, 27
John of Lancaster (later
        Duke of Bedford),
        42, 67, 83
    the character, 52–53, 85,
        89
    illustration of, 42
Johnson, Dr. Samuel, 39,
        48, 172
Jones, Griffith, 42
Jonson, Ben, 2, 5

Katherine (Queen to Henry
        VIII), 133, 136, 167
    the character, 135–45, 160,
        174
Katherine of Valois, 43,
        66–68, 104
    the character, 74, 165
    illustration of, 43

Keller, Elisabeth, 45
Kemble, John Philip, 163
*King John*, 2, 8, 10, 13, 15n,
        146–58, 162, 172, 173
    productions of, 165, 167,
        168
*King Lear*, 172, 176
King's Men, the, 2, 132.
        *See also* Lord Cham-
        berlain's Men


Lancaster. *See:* John of
        Gaunt; John of Lan-
        caster
Lancaster, House of, 29, 84–
        85, 103
    the fall of, 107, 118, 120
    versus the Yorkists, 83–
        85, 94–96, 105–108,
        128
language
    as comic deflation, 152
    in *Henry V*, 79
    of the histories, 176
    rhetorical, 131
    of the tragedies, 176
Laughton, Charles, 141
*Life and Death of King
        John, The. See King
        John*
*Life and Death of Richard
        the Second, The. See
        Richard II*
*Life and Death of Richard
        the Third, The. See
        Richard III*
*Life of King Henry the
        Eighth, The. See
        Henry VIII*

Lionel Duke of Clarence, 31n, 76, 84
London
  life in, 49, 50
  Shakespeare in, 3, 4, 5
Lord Chamberlain's Men, the, 1, 2, 5, 159. *See also* King's Men, the
Lord Chief Justice, 42, 55, 58, 62, 63
  illustration of, 42
Lowin, John, 164

*Macbeth*, 172, 176
Macbeth, 129, 154, 175–76
Magna Carta, the, 146, 148, 156, 165
Mansfield, Richard, 165
Margaret of Anjou (Queen to Henry VI), 81, 94–96, 103–104, 106–107, 118, 168–69
  the character, 92–93, 96–103, 109–115, 128–31, 160, 166
Marlowe, Christopher, 9
Mary Queen of Scots, 3, 139, 144
Mason, Brewster, 42
Memorial Theater, 166
Mercutio, 105
Meres, Frances, 2, 5
*Merry Wives of Windsor, The*, 8–9, 35
metaphors, 24–26, 27
Mistress Quickly, 31–32, 36, 42, 50, 57–59, 75
  illustration of, 41
Molière, Shakespeare compared to, 33

Montague, 114
Moore, Garry, 41
Moore, Richard, 42
morality in the histories, 10–11, 29
More, Sir Thomas, 11, 108, 119–20, 131, 144
  the character, 144
Mortimer, Edmund (Earl of March), 30–31, 30n–31n, 52, 66, 84, 86–87
  the character, 52, 86–87
Mowbray, Thomas, 16, 51–52
  the character, 16–29, 51–52

Naylor, Anthony, 42
Neville, Ralph (Earl of Westmoreland), 42, 67, 83
  the character, 52, 72
  illustration of, 42
New Place (Stratford), 2, 5
New York City, 165–66, 167
Norfolk, Duke of, 134, 144
Northampton, 105
Northumberland, Earl of, 31, 51
  the character, 33–34, 48–49, 60–61, 173
*Nothing like the Sun* (Burgess), 3

Old Vic, the, 167, 168
Olivier, Laurence, 79, 80, 166, 167
  illustrations of, 43, 47

Ophelia, 56
Oregon Festival Theater,
    168
Orléans (France), 88
*Othello*, 122, 175–76
Oxford, Earl of, 114

*Palladis Tamia* (Meres), 1,
    5
Pandulph, Cardinal, 147–49
    the character, 151–58
Peacock, Trevor, 42
Pepys, Samuel, 164
Percy, Henry (Hotspur),
        30–31, 33, 51, 164, 167
    the character, 32–39, 48–
        50, 53, 61, 160, 171,
        175
Percy rebellion, 30, 84
*Pericles*, 2, 167
Philip Faulconbridge (re-
        named Richard Plan-
        tagenet), 148, 150–58,
        167
Pistol, 41, 42, 44, 57, 75–76
    illustrations of, 41, 42, 44
Plantagenet, Richard. *See*
        Philip Faulconbridge;
        Richard Duke of
        York
Plutarch, 176
Poins, 31–32, 35, 40, 48, 49
    illustration of, 40
Polonius, 160
Pontrefact Castle, 17, 124
productions
    of the histories, 29, 164–
        70
    in Shakespeare's day, 29,
        159–63

Puritan Commonwealth,
    164

quarto editions, 6n, 6–7, 29
Quayle, Anthony, 167
Quiller-Couch, Arthur, 132

Redgrave, Michael, 167
Reformation, in England,
        12, 136, 157
Restoration, the, 164
*Richard II*, 10, 15n, 15–29,
        30, 173
    productions of, 2, 29,
        166–67, 168
Richard II (Richard of Bor-
        deaux), 15–16, 31n,
        83, 84, 95, 116, 124,
        128, 167
    the character, 16–29, 61,
        62, 160, 162, 171, 175
*Richard III*, 2, 12, 15n, 113,
        117–31, 164–65, 166,
        172
    film version of, 47, 166,
        167–68
    illustrations of, 46, 47
    productions of, 164–65,
        167, 168
Richard III (formerly Duke
        of Gloucester), 11,
        14, 15n, 46, 47, 83, 84,
        107–108, 117–20, 133,
        159, 163, 164–65
    the character, 103, 109–
        116, 120–31, 162, 175
    illustrations of, 46, 47
Richard Duke of York (for-
        merly second Earl of

Richard of York *(Cont'd)* Cambridge), 83, 84, 85, 95–96, 103–104, 105–106, 107
  the character, 86–87, 96–103, 108–111
Richard Earl of Cambridge (first), 66, 76, 84
Richardson, Ian, 46
Richardson, Ralph, 167, 168
Richard the Lionhearted, 146–49, 150, 157
Richmond, Earl of. *See* Henry VII
Riehle, Richard, 41
Rivers, Earl, 108, 118
  the character, 24, 128–30
*roman à clef*, 13
Roman Church, 10
*Romeo and Juliet*, 105
Rorvik, Alice, 41
Rouen (France), 89
Royal Shakespeare Theatre, 80, 167
Rutland, Earl of. *See* Edmund Earl of Rutland

St. Albans, 94, 103, 105, 106
St. Helier, Ivy, 43
Salisbury, Earl of (in *Henry VI*, Part One), 89, 162
Salisbury, Earl of (in *Henry VI*, Part Two), 95–96, 96–103, 106
Salisbury, Earl of (in *Richard II*), 16
satire, 76–77

Schroeder, Gregory Ward, 40
Second Blackfriars Theater, 2
*Second Part of King Henry the Fourth, The. See Henry IV*, Part Two
serious and the comic, the, convergence of, 32, 49, 74–75, 102, 159–60
Shakespeare, Anne. *See* Hathaway, Anne
Shakespeare, Hammet (son), 1, 4
Shakespeare, Judith (daughter), 1, 4
Shakespeare, Susanna (daughter), 1, 4
Shakespeare, William
  acting career of, 5
  birth of, 1, 3, 4
  burial of, 2, 3
  death of, 2, 3, 4–5
  father of, 4
  in London, 3, 4, 5
  marriage of, 1, 3, 4–5
  in Stratford, 3, 4, 6
  title received by, 4
Shakespeare quoted
  from *Henry IV*, Part One, 34–38 passim, 48
  from *Henry IV*, Part Two, 52–65 passim
  from *Henry V*, 69–78 passim, 163
  from *Henry VI*, Part One, 85–93 passim
  from *Henry VI*, Part Two, 97–102 passim
  from *Henry VI*, Part

Three, 108–116 passim
from *Henry VIII*, 134, 137–45 passim
from *King John*, 149, 152–58 passim
from *Richard II*, 19–28 passim
from *Richard III*, 120–30 passim
Shallow (Justice of the Peace), 59–60, 63, 167
Shaw, George Bernard, 172–73
Shore, Jane, 108
Shrewsbury, 30–35, 49, 51
Shylock, 56
Siddons, Sarah, 165
Silence (Justice of the Peace), 42, 59, 63
illustration of, 42
Sinclair, Upton, 172–73
Smith, James, 44
Somerset, Duke of. *See* Beaufort, Edmund (both); Beaufort, John
Spanish Armada, 10, 13
Stafford, Edward (third Duke of Buckingham), 133, 134–45
Stafford, Henry (second Duke of Buckingham), 46, 117, 119, 168
the character, 124–25, 128–30
illustration of, 46
Stafford, Humphrey (first Duke of Buckingham), 95–96, 96–103
stage, the
Elizabethan, 160–62
post-1660, 164, 165
Stanley, Lord Thomas (later Earl of Derby), 118
Stanley, Lord William, 108
Stratford, Connecticut, 168
Stratford, Ontario, 167, 168, 169
Stratford-on-Avon, 2, 5, 80, 166–67, 168, 169
Shakespeare in, 3, 4, 6
Stuarts, the, 2, 132–33, 132n, 145.
Suffolk, Earl of (in battle at Agincourt), 67
Suffolk, Earl of (later Duke of Suffolk), 95–96
the character, 86, 92–93, 96–103
Surrey, Earl of, 144
Swynford, Katherine, 83

Talbot, John, 90
Talbot, Lord, 14, 82, 87
the character, 87–92, 113
*Tartuffe* (Molière), 33
Taylor, Charles G., 44
*Tempest, The*, 6
tetralogy
the first. *See: Henry VI* (3 parts); *Richard III*
the second. *See: Henry IV* (2 parts); *Henry V; Richard II*

Tewkesbury, 107, 114

Thomas Duke of Clarence, 42

Thomas of Woodstock (Duke of Gloucester), 16, 95, 133

Timon of Athens, 175

Titus Andronicus, 8

Toby Belch (Sir), 35

Towton, 106

tragedies, 8

the histories compared to, 171–77

Tree, Beerbohm, 165–66

Troublesome Reign of John, King of England, The, 8, 148

Troyes (France), Treaty of, 67, 82

True Tragedy of Richard III, 9

Tudor, Owen, 104

Tudors, the, 11, 12, 104, 131, 134

Twelfth Night, 35, 49

Two Noble Kinsmen, The, 6

Ubi sunt, the, 130

Union of the two noble and illustre Families of Lancaster and Yorke, The (Hall), 11

unity, imagistic, 28–29

Warde, Frederick, 166

Wars of the Roses, 9, 83–85, 94–96, 105–108, 133

significance of, to Elizabethans, 116

Wars of the Roses, The, 168–69

Warwick, Earl of (in Henry IV, Part Two), 53

Warwick, Earl of (in Henry VI), 14, 95–96, 106–107

the character, 86, 96–103, 108–114

Westmoreland, Earl of. See Neville, Ralph

Williams (a soldier), 73, 79

Wolsey, Cardinal, 133, 136, 165, 167

the character, 134–45, 174

Woodville, Anthony, 118

Woodville, Elizabeth. See Elizabeth Woodville

Worcester, Earl of, 31

Wylton, Tom, 42

York, Archbishop of, 51–52

the character, 51–52, 61–62

York, Duke of. See: Edmund of Langley; Edward Duke of Aumerle; Richard Duke of York

York, House of, 85, 120

versus Lancastrians, 83–85, 94–96, 105–108, 128